How to Prepare For the STATE STANDARDS

VOL. 1

teacher

7th Grade Edition
By Todd Kissel
Warren Weaver
Dale Lundin

carney
EDUCATIONAL SERVICES

CARNEY EDUCATIONAL SERVICES
Helping Students Help Themselves

Special thanks to Rim Namkoong, our illustrator

This book is dedicated to:

The moms and dads who get up early and stay up late. You are the true heroes, saving our future, one precious child at a time.

All the kids who don't make the evening news. To the wide-eyed children, full of love, energy, and wonder. You are as close to perfection as this world will ever see.

TABLE OF CONTENTS

An Overview of the Standardized Test

Why do schools give this type of test? i
What subject areas does the test seek to measure? i
What do my child's test scores mean? ii
How valid are my child's test scores? ii

How Your Child Can Improve His/Her Score on Standardized Tests

The importance of reading iii
The importance of building a larger vocabulary iii
The importance of following written directions iv
    Select the best answer iv
    Answer the easy questions first v
    Eliminate any unreasonable answer choices v
    Do math questions on paper when necessary vi

LANGUAGE ARTS

Vocabulary Development and Word Recognition 1
Reading Comprehension and Analysis of Grade-Level Text 11
Writing Strategies, Organization and Focus 25
Literary Elements Including Response and Analysis 32
Writing Applications 39
Sentence Structure and Grammar Analysis 48

Answer Key 65

MATH

Number Sense – Scientific Notation 67
Number Sense – Communication Skills 70
Number Sense – Whole Number Powers 81
Number Sense – Convert Fractions 82
Number Sense – Use Decimals/Percents 84
Number Sense – Rational or Irrational 86
Number Sense – Terminating/Repeating 87
Number Sense – Converting – Decimals/Fractions 88
Number Sense – Percent Increase/Decrease 90

Number Sense – Discounts/Markups   91
Number Sense – Squares and Roots   93
Number Sense – Negative Exponents   94
Number Sense – Estimate Square Roots   95
Number Sense – Absolute Value   96
Algebra and Functions – Verbal to Problem   97
Algebra and Functions – Evaluate Expressions   100
Algebra and Functions – Simplify Expressions   101
Algebra and Functions – Algebraic Terminology   103
Algebra and Functions – Graphical Interpretation   104
Algebra and Functions – Positive/Negative Powers   106
Algebra and Functions – Monomials   108
Algebra and Functions – y=2n   109
Algebra and Functions – Slope   112
Algebra and Functions – Two-Step Equations   114
Algebra and Functions – Multi-Step Problems   116
Measurement and Geometry – Compare Measurements   118
Measurement and Geometry – Perimeter, Area, and Volume   120
Measurement and Geometry – Plane/Solid Shapes   123
Measurement and Geometry – Complex Figures   124
Measurement and Geometry – Scale Factor   126
Measurement and Geometry – Change Measurement   128
Measurement and Geometry – Coordinate Graph   131
Measurement and Geometry – Pythagorean Theorem   135
Measurement and Geometry – Congruency   137
Measurement and Geometry – 3-D Figures   139
Statistics, Data Analysis and Probability – Data Displays   141
Statistics, Data Analysis and Probability – Scatter Plot   144
Statistics, Data Analysis and Probability – Quartiles   146
Mathematical Reasoning – Evaluating Information   148
Mathematical Reasoning – Simpler Parts   151
Mathematical Reasoning – Diagrams, Models, etc.   153
Mathematical Reasoning – Approximation   155
Mathematical Reasoning – Inductive/Deductive   157
Mathematical Reasoning – Reasonable Answer   160
Answer Key   162

SOCIAL SCIENCE

World History and Geography: Medieval and Modern Times

The Causes and Effects of the Expansion and Subsequent Decline of
    the Roman Empire   166
The Origin, Growth, and Expansion of Islam in the Middle East and
    the Growth of Cities and Trade Routes in Asia, Africa, and Europe   169

China's Geography and its Impact on Political, Economic, and Religious
    Development; Emphasizing Inventions and Discoveries   172
Contributions of Sub-Saharan African Civilizations During the Medieval Period   175
The Development of Japan During the Medieval Period   179
The Development and Changes During the Middle Ages in Europe   182
The Mesoamerican and Andean Civilizations   187
The Renaissance: Origins, Growth, and Spread of Ideas and Achievements   191
The Reformation and its Historical Development   196
The Scientific Revolution and its Impact on Religious, Political, and
    Social Thought   199
The Age of Exploration, the Enlightenment, and the Age of Reason   202
Answer Key   206

SCIENCE

Life Science – Cell Biology   207
Life Science – Genetics   213
Life Science - Evolution   219
Earth Science   223
Structure and Function in Living Systems   228
Physical Science   234
Answer Key   240

An Overview of the Standardized Test

In the spring of 2005, almost all public school students in grades 2 through 11 took the state's required standardized test as part of the requirements for testing and reporting. This included non-English speaking children and most children who are in special education programs. The purpose behind this test is to provide both the school districts and parents with information about how their children are performing compared with other children from across the nation. Keep in mind that this is a test of basic skills. The test was written to assess the abilities of students only in specified areas of the curriculum. The exam is a standardized test. This means that ALL children across the state take the same tests in the same way. The directions given by teachers are the same, as are the amounts of time given to complete each testing section.

Why do schools give this type of test?

The test tells schools how well they are teaching basic skills which all students need to be successful in the future. Schools receive data about how their students did individually and by grade level. They use this information to help make teaching decisions. For example, if students at the fourth grade level all did well in the spelling section of the test, but didn't do as well in the reading comprehension section, those teachers may want to change the emphasis of their language arts program. Standardized tests are valuable, since they are an objective way to measure how successfully schools are delivering the basics. The idea behind standardizing the test is this: if every child takes the same tests in the same way, then it is a fair way to compare schools and districts. If, for example, one school gave all it's students an extra 5 hours to complete the test, then it would be an unfair advantage given to those children.

Each State Department of Education has taken extraordinary measures to ensure that all children get the same experience when taking the test. All testing materials are to be securely locked in classrooms or administrative offices when testing is not in progress. All teachers are discouraged from discussing test questions. Some districts even have non-teaching school employees act as proctors in classrooms to make sure that the testing procedures were being exactly followed. Schools want objective data about how well they are doing their jobs. Parents want this information as well.

What subject areas does the test seek to measure?

Students in grades 2-8 are tested in two main areas, language arts and math. The specific skills tested within language arts are reading comprehension, spelling, vocabulary, grammar, listening skills and study skills. The math sections of the test measures student mastery of the procedures such as math facts and computations, and then tests their ability to solve applied problems. The test contains sections that measure student knowledge in science and social studies. These two sections of the test were not given to 2nd through 8th grade students during the 2005 administration of the test.

The science and social science sections may be included as part of the testing program in the future years.

In grades 9 through 11, students were also tested in various reading and math skills. Additionally, these students were tested in science and social science.

What do my child's test scores mean?

In the fall, your child's school should have sent you a copy of his/her scores on the test. Scores for most students were reported on a form that shows National Percentile rankings. For example, if your child received a math problem solving percentile rank of 75, that means that s/he scored better that 75 percent of the national sampling of students at his/her grade level. Student performance on the test is measured by comparing your child's individual scores to scores from a national sample. This sample was created during a 1995 test given to students at various grade levels from across the country. The students selected for this 1995 test were representative of all students in the country. Their scores created a set of "norm scores". Scores of all other students taking the test can be compared against this set of scores. If your child got a percentile rank of 89 in spelling, they scored higher than 89 percent of the national sample. Obviously, this means your child ranks in the top 11 percent of students in the spelling section of the test. A percentile rank of 50 would place your child in the middle of the national sample. As you can see, schools want to ensure that parents get scores that accurately reflect their child's abilities, rather than coaching given by school personnel. In this system, it is important that all students compete on a level playing field.

How valid are my child's test scores?

This is where the controversy begins. Critics of the testing system point to the inclusion of non-English speaking students in the testing to make the case that results may not be reflective of a child's true abilities in the classroom. For example, if a Spanish-speaking child scores in the 15th percentile in study skills, it may be because s/he simply didn't understand the questions. Thus, his/her score is much lower than it would have been if s/he took the test in Spanish. Another undeniable fact about the statewide test results was this: children from wealthier suburban school districts performed much better on the test than did children from inner city school districts. Critics of the test contend that wealthier schools in the suburbs have many advantages such as computers or after-school programs that could ultimately help their students' scores on the test or any other testing program.

Even with all of this controversy, though, it is still clear that the test results do tell us a lot about how well children have learned the basic information which schools are supposed to teach. Looking at your child's scores can tell you about their strengths and weaknesses in each of the subject areas tested. Since the Department of Education is committed to continuing the test, you should use your child's current scores as a starting point for the future. You can, and should, assist your child in preparing to take the test in 2005 and beyond.

Certainly, the schools and teachers are primarily responsible for preparing your child for this test. Yet, parents have an important role to play. This book will give you some valuable tools you can use in helping your child do their best on this very important standardized test. It is the job of our nations schools to teach the material presented on the test, but your role as a reinforcer of skills and a supporter of your child's progress in school cannot be ignored.

How Your Child Can Improve Their Score On ANY Multiple Choice Standardized Test

Your child has entered an educational world that is run by standardized tests. Students take the Scholastic Aptitude Test (SAT) to help them get into college and the Graduate Record Examination (GRE) to help them get into graduate school. Other exams like the ACT and the PSAT are less famous, but also very important to your child's future success. Schools spend a great deal of time teaching children the material they need to know to do well on these tests, but very little time teaching children HOW to take these tests. This is a gap that parents can easily fill. To begin with, you can look for opportunities to strengthen your child's reading and vocabulary skills as well as their ability to follow detailed written directions.

The importance of reading:

Students who do well on standardized tests tend to be excellent readers. They read for pleasure frequently and have a good understanding of what they have read. You can help support your child as a reader by helping them set aside a regular time to read each and every day. As you may know, children tend to be successful when they follow an established pattern of behavior. Even 15-20 minutes spent reading a magazine or newspaper before bedtime will help. Children should read both fiction and non-fictional material at home, as well as at school. Ask your child about what they have read. Help them to make connections between a book they are currently reading and a movie or a television show they have recently seen. THE BOTTOM LINE: Children who read well will do better on the test than children who do not. There is written material in all sections of the test that must be quickly comprehended. Even the math sections have written information contained in each question.

The importance of building a larger vocabulary:

As you may know, children who read well and who read often tend to have a large vocabulary. This is important since there is an entire section of the test that is devoted exclusively to the use of vocabulary words. You can support your child in attempting to improve their vocabulary by encouraging them to read challenging material on a regular basis. The newspaper is a good place to start. Studies have shown that many newspaper articles are written on a 4th to 5th grade reading level! Help your child to use new and more difficult words both in their own conversations and in their writings. If you use an advanced vocabulary when speaking to your child, don't be surprised if they begin to incorporate some of the new words into their daily speech. To be honest, one of the most immediate ways to judge the intelligence of anyone is in their use of language. Children are aware of this too. THE BOTTOM LINE: Children who have an expansive vocabulary will do better on the test than children who do not. Find as many ways as possible to help build new words into your child's speech and writing.

The importance of following written directions:

The test is a teacher-directed test. Teachers tell students how to complete each section of the test, and give them specific examples that are designed to help them understand what to do. However, teachers are not allowed to help students once each test has begun. The written script for teachers seems to repeat one phrase continually: "READ THE DIRECTIONS CAREFULLY". This is certainly not an accident. Students face a series of questions that cannot be answered correctly unless the student clearly understands what is being asked for. Help your child by giving them a series of tasks to complete at home in writing. Directions should be multi-step and should be as detailed as possible without frustrating your child. For example: "Please take out the trash cans this afternoon. Place all the bottles and cans in the blue recycling bin and place all the extra newspapers that are stacked in the garage in the yellow recycling bin." If children are able to follow these types of directions and are able to reread to clarify what is being asked, they will be at a tremendous advantage when it comes to the test.
THE BOTTOM LINE: Children who are able to follow a series of detailed, written directions will have a tremendous advantage over those who are unable to do so.

All of the previous suggestions are designed to be used before the test is actually given to help your child improve in some basic test-taking skills. Here are some strategies that you can teach your child to use once they are taking the test:

1. SELECT THE BEST ANSWER.

The test, like many multiple-choice tests, isn't designed for children to write their own answers to the questions. They will fill in a bubble by the four answer choices and select the BEST possible answer. Reading the question carefully is quite important, since the question may contain key words needed to select the correct answer. For example:

The first President of the United States was

a. John Adams
b. James Madison
c. George Washington
d. Thomas Jefferson

The correct answer is, of course, "c". Students would need to read the question carefully and focus on the key work in the question: "first". All of the names listed were Presidents of the United States early in our history, but only choice "c" contains the name of our first President. Looking for key words like "least" or "greater" will help your child to select the best answer from among the choices given.

2. ANSWER THE EASY QUESTIONS FIRST.

The test contains a series of timed tests. Children who waste time on a difficult question found at the beginning of a test may run out of time before they finish the entire test. A good strategy is to skip anything that seems too difficult to answer immediately. Once your child has answered every "easy" question in the section, they can go back through the test and spend more time working on the more time-consuming questions. If students are given only 30 minutes to answer 25 reading vocabulary questions, they shouldn't spend much more than a minute on each one. Wasting four or even five minutes on one question is not a good idea, since it reduces the amount of time your child will have to work on the rest of the test. Once time runs out, that's it! Any questions left unanswered will be counted wrong when the test is machine scored. Working on the easier questions first will allow your child to make the best use of the allowed time.

3. ELIMINATE ANY UNREASONABLE ANSWER CHOICES.

No matter how intelligent your child is, it is inevitable that they will come to test questions that they find too difficult to answer. In this situation, the best thing to do is to make an "educated guess". If students can eliminate one or more of the answer choices given, they have a much greater chance of answering the question correctly.

For example:

Select the word below that means the same as the underlined word:

Jennifer became <u>enraged</u> when she found out her diary had been read.

> a. mournful
> b. furious
> c. pleased
> d. depressed

Even if your child didn't know that "b" is the best answer choice, they could certainly eliminate choice "c" from consideration. Clearly, Jennifer would not be "pleased" to find out her diary had been read.

4. DO MATH QUESTIONS ON PAPER WHEN NECESSARY.

The math sections of the test cause children problems because several of the answer choices seem like they could be correct. The only way to select the best answer choice for some math questions is to do the math calculation on scratch paper. The answer choices given for these questions are written to discourage guessing.

For example:

Eileen has saved $3245 to buy a car. Her aunt gave her another $250 as a gift. How much does she have in all?

    a. $3595
    b. $4495
    c. $3495
    d. $3485

The correct answer is "c", but it is hard to select the correct answer because all of the answer choices seem similar. The best way to determine the correct answer would be to add $3245 and $250 on scratch paper.

> If you work with your child with these simple strategies, you will find that they will approach these tests with confidence, rather than with anxiety. Teach your child to prepare and then to approach the test with a positive attitude. They should be able to say to themselves; " I know this stuff, I'll do a great job today."

LANGUAGE ARTS

Content Cluster: VOCABULARY DEVELOPMENT AND WORD RECOGNITION

Objective: To assess knowledge of (1), idioms and analogies; (2), Greek, Latin, and Anglo-Saxon roots and affixes; and (3), clarification of word meanings.

Parent Tip: Reading continues to be a critical component of education, and life in general. By using context, roots, and other usage clues, the student will expand the skills associated with vocabulary building, thereby improving reading. The following are several activities that provide opportunities to improve students reading, writing, and speaking vocabularies.

Directions: In the following groups of words, identify the idioms.

45/60

1. in a teasing manner; not serious

   a. cleaning his tongue
   b. a sore tongue
   c. tongue in cheek
   d. bit a tongue

2. speaking without much purpose

   a. chewing the fat
   b. chewing some fat
   c. trimming the fat
   d. heating the fat

3. initial action, usually between two persons

   a. break through the ice
   b. water over ice
   c. break the ice
   d. melt the ice

4. not a particularly clean or upscale restaurant

   a. ate with a greasy spoon
   b. found a greasy spoon
   c. cleaned the greasy spoon
   d. ate at a greasy spoon

5. human reactions

   a. pink polka dots
   b. white as a sheet
   c. green with envy
   d. a and b
   e. b and c

Read the following poem and identify the best answers to the questions.

"Dripping with silver,
They stand silent
Like hushed monoliths,
In a world awash with moonlight,

And the night sings on,
And the summer dawn comes,
And the sun replaces the silver
    with haloes of gold.

Ah! I know not which is more lovely,
The moonlight or the dawnlight
On poplars standing silent
    in the hush of their beauty."

                  L. Weaver

6. The first verse in the poem contains

   a. a metaphor
   b. a simile
   c. alliteration
   d. none of the above

7. The third verse in the poem contains

   a. a metaphor
   b. a simile
   c. an association
   d. none of the above

8. In the poem, what is being compared?

   a. moonlight and light of dawn
   b. poplars and night
   c. poplars and monoliths
   d. a and b
   e. a and c

9. Which of the following sentences contains a simile?

    a. Many of the fans thought that the previous evening's show was more exciting.
    b. Few among the eager media members were meticulous with the details.
    c. The middle distance runner ran like a gazelle.
    d. none of the above

10. A metaphor is

    a. a comparison, that uses like or as.
    b. a comparison, that uses a definition.
    c. a comparison that does not use like or as.
    d. none of the above

11. Which of the following sentences contains a metaphor?

    a. The bedraggled bobcat, imitating a drowned rat, hunted aimlessly in the rain.
    b. In the forest, the sounds were as soft as the falling snow.
    c. With large eyes, the kitten pounced upon the moving bug.
    d. none of the above

Choose the word root that gives the meaning of each of these words.

12. missionary
    a. mission
    b. mis
    c. ary
    d. onary

13. reversal
    a. reverse
    b. versal
    c. rev
    d. vers

14. graduate
    a. grad
    b. graduation
    c. ate
    d. none of the above

15. intolerable
    a. into
    b. able
    c. tolerate
    d. lerat

16. magnitude
    a. magnus
    b. tude
    c. mag
    d. magnify

17. promote
    a. pro
    b. omo
    c. romote
    d. mot

18. millipede
    a. mile
    b. ped
    c. mille
    d. none of the above

19. transport
    a. trans
    b. sport
    c. port
    d. tran

Directions: In the following exercises, select the correct choice for the meaning of the prefix or suffix.

20. exfoliate, extrapolate, extract, explain, excommunicate, exhale

    a. small
    b. again
    c. out of, from
    d. through

21. glamorous, ominous, tumultuous, contiguous, contagious

    a. without
    b. within
    c. characterized by
    d. around

22. knowledgeable, believable, comfortable, biodegradable, convertible

    a. capable of, worthy of
    b. around
    c. because of
    d. through

23. proponent, prologue, protagonist, provide

    a. not
    b. yield
    c. life
    d. before, in front of

24. codify, amplify, verify, typify, nullify

    a. movement
    b. surround
    c. make into
    d. ability to

25. legalize, fossilize, digitize, acclimatize, brutalize, itemize

    a. cause of
    b. cause to be
    c. native of
    d. around

26. recall, redundant, react, reduce, rebirth, rebate

    a. see
    b. again
    c. not
    d. without

27. transmit, transport, transaction, transformation, transparent

    a. across
    b. down
    c. receive
    d. understand

28. unmitigated, undeveloped, uneducated, unforeseen, uninhabited

    a. before
    b. come from
    c. instead of
    d. not

Identify the word meaning that is the same or most nearly the same as the word that is given.

29. implode

    a. to collapse violently inward
    b. to annihilate
    c. to break apart
    d. to discover

30. pessimistic

    a. positive
    b. expecting the best
    c. emphasizing adverse conditions
    d. understanding

31. acquisition

    a. the act of gaining control or possession
    b. the ability to recover
    c. the ability to act
    d. recommendation to behave properly

32. distraught

    a. disgusted
    b. able to foretell future events
    c. being affected with doubt; having mental conflict
    d. disturbed

33. remembrance

    a. ability to remember
    b. a memory of a person or event
    c. an object that serves to keep a memory
    d. a and b
    e. b and c

34. avalanche

    a. a storm with high winds
    b. sometimes violent shaking of the earth
    c. a mass of snow, ice, and rock falling swiftly down a mountain
    d. boat launch area

35. catalyst

    a. agent of change; special substance
    b. a listing of material
    c. a secret agent
    d. a tragic event

36. incredible

    a. severe forecast
    b. most likely
    c. a person with unique ideas
    d. unbelievable

37. semantics

    a. using synonyms to find meanings of words
    b. study of meanings and forms of words
    c. a sea animal
    d. study of reading comprehension

38. hysterical

    a. emotional excitability
    b. uncontrolled laughter
    c. none of the above
    d. a and b

39. propaganda

    a. natural probability for success
    b. spreading ideas, information, or rumors to further one's cause
    c. ideas that agree with the government
    d. appearing in court

40. retaliate

    a. an unfair deed
    b. an average attempt
    c. to deface
    d. to repay or get revenge

Directions: In the following sentences, choose the correct context clue that helps unlock the meaning of the underlined word.

41. Having scored three touchdowns in the all-star game, Ryan culminated his **illustrious** and outstanding high school career.

    a. example
    b. restatement
    c. contrast

42. Unlike many early civilizations who believed in many gods, the Muslims, Jews, and Christians were **monotheistic**.

    a. example
    b. restatement
    c. contrast

43. While hiking in the backcountry, Julie was bitten by a bug that was barely **discernable**, or able to be seen.

    a. example
    b. restatement
    c. contrast

44. **Gesticulating** wildly, the stranded motorist waved his arms frantically as he shouted to the passersby to stop.

    a. example
    b. restatement
    c. contrast

45. Princess Diana was known to perform **humanitarian** deeds. Her efforts to eliminate the suffering of victims of land mines throughout Europe were commendable.

    a. example
    b. restatement
    c. contrast

46. The **compassionate** boss showed some sympathy for the late worker.

    a. example
    b. restatement
    c. contrast

47. **Superfluous** decorations for the reception were contrary to what was considered essential.

    a. example
    b. restatement
    c. contrast

Choose the best answer.

48. Which of the following indicates that an object is not moving?

    a. stationery
    b. superior
    c. prudent
    d. stationary

49. Which of the following words shows a characteristic of a person who always puts forth effort toward a task?

    a. consensus
    b. conscientious
    c. conscious
    d. concentric

50. Which of the following words indicates ability to eat both animal and vegetable substances?

    a. omnivorous
    b. ominous
    c. omnipotent
    d. omen

51. Which of the following words would indicate the strongest wind force?

    a. breeze
    b. gale
    c. light wind
    d. hurricane

52. If something is *irresistible* it is

    a. uncertain how to act.
    b. impossible to withstand.
    c. impossible to bring together.
    d. not rational.

53. Which of the following words implies a small bit or portion?

    a. snippet
    b. summary
    c. preface
    d. succinct

54. A person who is *ravenous* is usually

    a. eager to start a project.
    b. attractive.
    c. confused.
    d. very eager for food.

55. Rainfall occurs *sporadically* in many areas of the West. This means:

    a. frequently
    b. regularly
    c. on an infrequent basis
    d. during the winter

56. Parrots, flying above the trees produced a raucous, harsh sound or a

   a. symphony
   b. cacophony
   c. harmony
   d. monotony

57. Football announcers occasionally refer to the ball and a "*fortuitous*" bounce; in other words,

   a. an unfortunate bounce.
   b. an unpleasant bounce.
   c. an immutable bounce.
   d. a lucky or fortunate bounce.

58. The candidate's remarks on health care were *misconstrued*.

   a. not interpreted correctly
   b. insulting
   c. not peaceful
   d. none of the above

59. Although insecticide was used, this species of millipede was fairly *innocuous*.

   a. dangerous
   b. poisonous
   c. producing no injury
   d. common

60. Roman banquets were *gastronomic* productions.

   a. having to do with glands of the stomach
   b. insatiable
   c. enormous
   d. having to do with consuming food

Content Cluster: READING COMPREHENSION AND ANALYSIS OF GRADE-LEVEL TEXT, EMPHASIZING INFORMATIONAL MATERIALS

Objective: To evaluate student's knowledge of: (1) the differences in structure and purpose among categories of informational materials; (2) information found in a variety of materials; (3) cause-and-effect patterns; (4) assessing an author's point of view, noting accuracy, appropriateness, bias and stereotyping.

Parent Tip: Any and all reading is recommended. Before beginning to read, it is advisable for your student to scan the passage to ascertain the type of material to be examined. Is it fiction or non-fiction? Is the author familiar? Has your student read any other books by the author? A suggestion for recreational reading is to keep a list of the books you and your student have read and an idea or two about each of the books. If the reading is non-fiction, a biography for instance, or a textbook, you are probably reading for information. The reading of informational materials is a focus of this section.

Directions: Choose the best answer for the following questions.

1. To find information relating to congressional candidates and their campaigns for the upcoming election you should look in

   a. newspapers.
   b. social science books.
   c. political science books.
   d. magazines.
   e. both a and d

2. Information that compares the American Revolution with the French Revolution would most likely be located in

   a. manuals.
   b. newspapers.
   c. textbooks.
   d. pamphlets.

3. To set up a computer for the first time, you should look in

   a. the owners' manual.
   b. newspapers.
   c. textbooks.
   d. magazines.

4. Sections are an organizational pattern most often found in

    a. newspapers.
    b. textbooks.
    c. manuals.
    d. a and b only
    e. a and c only

5. In the back of some social science books, a list of place names used in the book may be found. This listing is called a

    a. glossary
    b. index
    c. gazetteer
    d. dictionary

6. What is the name given to the part of the newspaper in which people can write to express their views?

    a. opinion
    b. editorial
    c. letters
    d. op-ed
    e. all of the above

7. Tables of contents are listing of main topics within a printed document. Which of the following are likely to have one?

    a. newspaper
    b. manual
    c. textbook
    d. all of the above
    e. a and c only

Directions: Read this letter and answer the following questions.

CITY OF OAKWOOD

NOTICE OF PUBLIC HEARING

Case Number: Conditional Use Permit #533

Applicant: Sports Warehouse

Site: 1547 North Ridgeview Drive

NOTICE IS HEREBY GIVEN that on Tuesday, March 24, the Planning Commission of the City of Oakwood will hold a public hearing to consider an application for a Conditional Use Permit to allow the building of a parking structure at the above location. All local zoning regulations will be in effect.

The hearing will be held in the Council Chambers of City Hall at 6:30 p.m. The City Hall is located at 2304 White Bear Road. Agenda items for the hearing will be placed in order the week of March 16. Persons interested in speaking will be given the opportunity. Permit application materials are open for review during business hours at City Hall.

This project requires compliance with the California Environmental Quality Act. The Environmental Impact Report will be available for review as well.

If you challenge the Permit action or environmental impact in court, you may raise only those issues discussed at this public hearing, or by written correspondence delivered to the Planning Commission at, or before the public hearing.

Dennis Anderson
Director, Planning Commission

8. What is the correct address of the proposed parking structure?

    a. 1547 North Ridgecrest Drive
    b. 2304 White Bear Road
    c. 2416 Ocean Crest Lane
    d. 1547 North Ridgeview Drive

9. What is the purpose of the letter?
    a. to protest the possible construction of a parking structure
    b. to announce the date of a public hearing on the construction of a parking structure
    c. to set the court date for legal action on the parking structure
    d. to allow people a chance to speak on the proposed parking structure
    e. b and d

10. If the permit action is challenged in court, a person may raise the following issues.
    a. those which were written and brought to the Planning Commission
    b. those which deal with the parking structure
    c. those which were discussed at the meeting
    d. a and b only
    e. a and c only

11. The main purpose of the Planning Commission in the City of Oakwood is to

    a. oversee construction projects that impact people in the city.
    b. plan and build construction projects for the city.
    c. design construction projects for the city.
    d. have meetings.

12. If a person wanted to see the permit application, he should

    a. go to the hearing.
    b. call the Planning Commission.
    c. visit City Hall and ask to review the application.
    d. contact the Planning Commission Director.

YOSEMITE NATIONAL PARK
GENERAL MANAGEMENT PLAN

[Yosemite National Park is located in Central California on the western side of the Sierra Nevada Mountains. The following excerpts were taken from "Yosemite's 1980 General Management Plan"]

The mission of the National Park Service is to "...conserve the scenery and the natural and historic objects and wild life therein and to provide for the enjoyment of same in such manner ... as will leave them unimpaired for the enjoyment of future generations."

Soon after non-Indians first encountered Yosemite Valley in 1851, tourists started coming to see the Valley's "scenic wonders." There were 147 visitors in 1864, 623 in 1868, 1,735 in 1870, and over 4,000 in 1886. Visitation has continued to climb, and by the late 1990's, nearly four million people (and their cars) visited Yosemite each year. To meet the needs of the increasing visitation, development also increased in the park over the years. By 1980, it was recognized that Yosemite Valley had become congested with more than a thousand buildings, that the Valley floor was bisected by approximately 30 miles of roads, and that the Yosemite Valley experience of many visitors had become one of crowds and traffic jams.

The five broad goals of the general management plan for Yosemite are to:
- reclaim priceless natural beauty
- reduce traffic congestion
- allow natural processes to prevail
- reduce crowding
- promote visitor understanding and enjoyment

Ecological restoration involves human manipulation of sites to restore soils, topography, hydrology, vegetation, and disturbance patterns to pre-impact conditions. Restoration work begins with research: studying early photographs and maps of the area to be restored, and looking at soils, hydrology, and vegetation patterns in adjacent, undisturbed sites.

The National Park Service seeks to perpetuate the best possible air quality in parks because of its critical importance to visitor enjoyment, human health, scenic vistas, and the preservation of natural systems and cultural resources. Vegetation, visibility, water quality, wildlife, and most other elements of the park's environment are sensitive to air pollution. Sources of air emissions in Yosemite Valley include vehicles, boilers and furnaces, generators, campfire smoke, residential wood stoves and fireplaces, and prescribed burning. Park management is considering measures to mitigate emissions from these sources.

The National Park Service also recognizes the importance of cultural resources located within Yosemite Valley. Entities that would receive protection under every alternative would include known American Indian burial areas, the Yosemite Village Historic District, and National Historic Landmarks such as The Ahwahnee Hotel.

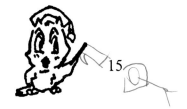

Directions: Choose the best answer to the following questions.

13. This article was written because

    a. Many people wanted to close Yosemite National Park to visitors.
    b. There were too many visitors to the Park in the late 1990's.
    c. Bears and other animals are a threat to the visitors.
    d. There is concern for the animals, plants, scenery, etc. in the Park because of too many visitors and the pollution that they cause.

14. According to this article, what is the main reason that the number of people and cars in the Park is a problem?

    a. Cars are noisy and scare the animals.
    b. There are not enough parking places near the shops and restaurants.
    c. The number of cars entering the Park affects air quality.
    d. People are usually not considerate and create a lot of litter and noise.

15. Cultural resources located within the Park would include:

    a. The Ahwahnee Hotel
    b. The Merced River
    c. Campfire programs and ranger talks
    d. none of the above

16. Because of the increased visitation in the Park

    a. Many animals died from problems relating to pollution.
    b. There were so many people and cars that roads became crowded and often there are traffic jams.
    c. Park employees had to ride bicycles to work to cut down on the traffic.
    d. Campers were encouraged not to have campfires at night.

17. If we do not do something to preserve our National Parks

    a. Our ancestors will be unhappy with us.
    b. Many people will lose their jobs as rangers, cooks, and tour guides.
    c. More and more people will visit the parks annually.
    d. Future generations will not be able to enjoy wildlife and vegetation as it used to be.

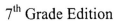

GHOST TOWNS OF THE AMERICAN WEST

(Courtesy of ghost town author Philip Varney)

Ghost towns are empty reminders of gold and silver mining bonanzas that brought thousands of hopeful dreamers to the American West in the late 1800's. Today the boards of their buildings bleach in the sun, their tin roofs bend and clatter in the wind, and their cemeteries rest silently on forgotten hillsides.

A hundred years ago, these towns were spectacularly alive, overrun with miners and merchants, clergymen and saloonkeepers, lawmakers and lawbreakers – and very few women. But the towns they created were destined to fail, because when the gold and silver that fueled the excitement was gone, the settlements were doomed. When the news of another mineral discovery reached a declining town, people quickly gathered most of their possessions and hurried to the next boom town. The community they left behind became a ghost town, sometimes littered with the possessions that the departing townspeople couldn't carry.

Today there are hundreds of ghost towns in the West. Most are only mere traces on the landscape or are remembered only because they still are named on a map. But every state in the western United States has ghost towns that are well worth visiting.

A true ghost town has two characteristics: the population has dramatically decreased, and the initial reason for settlement, almost always a mine, no longer supports the community. The pure ghost town is completely deserted, but most have a few residents who try to keep the buildings and their contents from disappearing due to the biggest threat to ghost towns: souvenir-seekers and vandals. If, then, a ghost town can have residents, how will you know if you're in one? A large majority of the buildings will be run-down and vacant, and community buildings like schools, churches, and courthouses will either be empty or used for other purposes. If a town of several thousand people has decreased to a couple of hundred, it's a ghost town.

Bodie, California, is a perfect example of a ghost town. It began when a huge deposit of gold was discovered in the 1870's, and thousands of people rushed to the area to make their fortunes. Bodie soon became known as one of California's most lawless places. When one little girl was told by her parents that they were moving to Bodie, that

evening the parents overheard the little girl say in her evening prayer, "Goodbye, God, I'm going to Bodie." But the gold gave out quickly, and Bodie was practically empty only a few years after it was founded. Today it is one of the largest ghost towns in the country, with 170 buildings still standing. Some houses have dishes on the dining room tables, and the schoolhouse still features desks, textbooks, and cutout Easter bunny decorations on the wall. The school's clock has no hands – almost as it time has stopped.

Bodie is now a California State Park, with rangers there to prevent visitors from removing items or vandalizing the town. In addition, specially trained carpenters work to keep Bodie in what is known as a state of "arrested decay," which means that buildings are protected, repaired, and propped up if necessary, but they are not restored to try to make Bodie look the way it did in the 1870's. Instead, it looks like what it is: America's best ghost town.

Tens of thousands of tourists visit the West's ghost towns every year. For many of them, the chance to see an abandoned town is a way to experience the West's exciting past in a very personal way: If you can stand where history was once made, it's almost as it you have projected yourself back in time.

QUESTIONS

18. Most ghost towns were originally settled because

    a. the railroad came through a new area
    b. gold or silver were discovered nearby
    c. people seeking adventure came to a new place
    d. criminals were looking for a place to escape the law

19. Of all the people who settled in the bonanza towns of the American West, the ones you would likely find in the fewest numbers were

    a. miners
    b. saloon keepers
    c. lawmen
    d. women

20. Bonanza towns became ghost towns because

    a. people left when gold and silver deposits gave out
    b. citizens left when the towns became too big
    c. townspeople left when the railroad didn't stop there anymore
    d. criminals left when lawmakers arrived

21. How many western states have ghost towns worth visiting?

    a. one
    b. several
    c. most of them
    d. every single one

22. What is the biggest threat to ghost towns?

    a. severe winds
    b. souvenir hunters and vandals
    c. land developers
    d. floods

23. The little girl who made the evening prayer was

    a. looking forward to moving to Bodie because it was a "big city".
    b. aware that God would help protect her on her journey.
    c. afraid that God would not be there because it was such a lawless place
    d. afraid that Bodie would be a bad place to live.

24. Bodie is typical of a ghost town in that it

    a. grew fast when gold was discovered, but died quickly when the gold was gone.
    b. grew slowly as people moved to the area, but died quickly because of a highly contagious disease.
    c. never really amounted to much as a town and then became pretty much forgotten.
    d. was a lawless town in the beginning, but then eventually became a quiet place to live.

25. Bodie is one of the West's best-preserved ghost towns because it is

    a. so far away from civilization that very few people know where it is.
    b. on private property so no one can disturb it.
    c. a state park so no one can visit it.
    d. a state park and has rangers to protect it.

26. In Bodie, specially trained carpenters try to

    a. construct buildings that are similar to ones that stood there in the 1870's.
    b. protect and repair buildings to make them stay as they are now.
    c. make them decay.
    d. make Bodie look just as it did in the 1870's.

CASTLES

The Middle Ages were a time of great change in Western Europe. This period beginning with the fall of Rome in a.d. 476, saw people moving quickly in roaming bands of locally governed groups, chasing each other through the country as they escaped the Huns. There was little protection. Charlemagne and some of his predecessors were able to arrange some stability. However, after his rule, a second wave of invaders including the Vikings and the Magyars attacked people living in the northern and western parts of Europe. It was here during the ninth century that many people began to turn to lords and their fortified complexes known as castles. From this point, castles spread to Germany, Austria, Italy, and other parts of France.

The development of castles parallels societal forces at work during this period that lasted until the 1500's. Early castle structures were simple constructions built primarily from wood and earth. These were called motte and bailey castles. They had a main building or tower built on raised earth or a mound surrounded by a fence called a palisade. Both the tower and other buildings were constructed of wood with plaster covering a wooden frame.

Naturally these types of castles, although easy to construct were unable to provide much real protection from invaders. Additional defenses were designed near ocean coastline, or close to other water sources as rivers. Castle builders could dig ditches and use the nearby water to fill the ditches, creating moats. These structures allowed greater protection for the castle dwellers.

The development in England was vastly different. Despite the fact that there were few castles in place, Alfred the Great drove away repeated attacks by both Danes and Vikings. In 1066, William, Duke of Normandy invaded England. The lack of strong fortification made his task somewhat easier. After his defeat of Harold at the Battle of Hastings, William encountered little opposition.

Obviously, these earth and wooden structures were not strong. Stone began to be used as the main construction material. Initially only the keeps, or strong holds of the castles were built with stone, but over time castles were built entirely in this fashion. Affording more protection, these structures evolved into military machines, that, when manned by several dozen men, could hold off an entire army.

Additional embellishments such as a portcullis, and battlement structures including crenels (openings) and merlons in a square tooth pattern were added. Other defense mechanisms such as concentric enclosures with gatehouses, which were staggered, allowed the archers multiple angles with which to bombard the attacking force.

It is somewhat ironic that a number of important refinements in castle building were introduced to Europe by crusaders returning from the holy lands. Castle construction in Europe was already an art form by the time the first nobles and knights left on the First Crusade in 1095. What these warriors did not expect to see was established types of castles already in existence in the Middle East.

Castles built by the Muslims had unique elements that aided their defense. These castles were likely built on high points of land with the inner bailey backed against the steep side. This allowed the main defense to face the more gradual side. New brotherhoods of knights with help from Turks and Greeks designed several castles to help preserve crusader states in Syria and Israel. One castle survived a number of sieges. This technology was transported immediately to Western Europe, with newly designed castles being constructed by nobles as soon as they returned home from the Crusades.

Another major technique, which was acquired in the Holy Land, was the round tower. Towers in general afforded archers the opportunity to aim along the face of walls. Rectangular towers had several disadvantages, however. The outside wall of the tower was somewhat protected from defensive fire allowing attackers to use battering rams or siege towers with which to hammer the outside wall of the tower. Similarly, diggers could tunnel under the tower, and by removing dirt and debris, would collapse the tower affording easy access to the castle interior.

Towers of the round design could more easily ward off these types of attacks while affording archers a wider range of vision. Round towers were stronger in withstanding catapults and later, fire from cannons and guns. The round tower design did make its way through Europe at a somewhat more gradual rate.

As the social and political forces that brought about the creation of castle fortresses changed, so too did their impact on the decline of these structures. Improved warfare techniques, specifically the introduction of gunpowder to Europe, enabled attacking forces to capture castles, particularly if the walls themselves were not solid. However, some castles were able to withstand these attacks, and indeed had mounted cannons on platforms for defense. Henry VIII designed several castles in this fashion. By the end of the sixteenth century castle building had diminished.

Economic factors as well as basic military tactics hastened their decline. Large-scale economic changes had taken place throughout Europe. By the sixteenth and seventeenth centuries, colonies had been established in the New World. Extensive worldwide trade was in place, and wealthy European merchants were competing for monopolies in gold, and spices. European towns had grown steadily into cities.

Politically, the power of the lords had declined for centuries, being replaced by monarchies and nation states. Taxes were collected and the funds used to support large armies of mercenary soldiers, which fought against other European nations for supremacy. The capture of a castle was not as important as the capture of an army.

While some of the classic castles fell into disrepair, castle building continued in Europe. During the eighteenth and nineteenth centuries, these structures looked different and were built for other reasons. "Fairy tale" castles were designed and built for beauty and comfort rather than defense. Thus, as Europe evolved, so too did the castle. From an earth and wooden affair into a stone war machine, the castle has become a monument to the medieval European period.

27. During the early Middle Ages, groups of people such as the Franks, the Ostrogoths, and many others traveled in haste through Europe to avoid _____, a fierce, warlike tribe from Asia.

    a. the Mongols
    b. the Huns
    c. the Muslims
    d. the Anglo-Saxons

28. Because the Vikings and Magyars attacked various areas of Europe,

    a. people living there sought protection from the kings.
    b. people traveled to England, where they were protected.
    c. people living there turned to feudal lords for protection.
    d. kings built huge armies to defend themselves.

29. Some of the earliest castles were called motte and bailey. They were best characterized by

    a. a stone keep inside the castle wall.
    b. a large mote.
    c. a tower built on a mound of earth.
    d. concentric enclosures.

30. Builders used water from rivers to fill moats. The purpose of the moats was to

    a. afford an area for the lord's navy to practice maneuvers.
    b. give greater protection for people in the castle.
    c. allow a place for alligators to inhabit.
    d. help irrigate the fields.

31. William's conquest of England was made somewhat easier by the fact that

    a. there were few castles in England at the time.
    b. no castles had moats.
    c. the castles were destroyed by attackers.
    d. the castles did not afford much protection.

32. The author sees changes in castle construction occurring

    a. as stronger materials began to be used.
    b. as castle towers were built taller.
    c. other defense mechanisms were developed.
    d. a and c
    e. a and b

33. The author found it interesting that

    a. Crusaders found elaborate castles in Egypt.
    b. Crusaders used building techniques from the Middle East on European castles after they returned home.
    c. castle development in the Middle East was advanced.
    d. b and c
    e. a and c

34. In statements in the article, the author indicates bias by saying the Crusaders were surprised to see established castles in the Middle East. The author implies that

    a. people of other cultures couldn't have the knowledge necessary to build castles.
    b. castles could be built by anyone.
    c. Crusaders could not build castles as well as Turks.
    d. castle design was seriously absent in the Holy Land.

35. Which of the following choices was not a defense mechanism added to European castles?

    a. a portcullis
    b. crenels and merlons
    c. stone keeps
    d. catapults
    e. gatehouses

36. Rectangular towers were situated along walls and on corners to give archers angles along the walls. Their disadvantage was that

    a. the archers could not see along the walls.
    b. a "blind spot" was created which allowed the enemy a place to attack.
    c. the archers were open to attack from all sides.
    d. a and b
    e. b and c

37. Round towers were an improvement over the earlier type because

    a. they could more easily deflect catapults and later cannons.
    b. they could withstand digging efforts more easily.
    c. they eliminated the "blind spot".
    d. all of the above
    e. a and c

38. Economic factors which helped castles diminish in importance were

    a. growth of towns and the establishment of worldwide trade.
    b. increased power of the kings.
    c. improved craftsmanship.
    d. improved crop rotation methods.

39. Which of these factors was **not** important in the decline of castles?

    a. introduction of gunpowder to Europe
    b. importance of armies
    c. increased power of kings
    d. increased power of lords

40. For the author, the decline of castles parallels

    a. the education of European people.
    b. the social, economic, and political changes taking place in Europe.
    c. the introduction of new methods of castle building from the Middle East.
    d. a and b
    e. a and c

Content Cluster: WRITING STRATEGIES, ORGANIZATION AND FOCUS

Objective: To evaluate the student's knowledge of: (1) the organization of essays; (2) transitions between sentences; (3) the use of anecdotes, facts and specific examples; and (4) the use of proper research formats.

Parent Tip: Observation is the key. As a person reads more often, she becomes aware of strategies that writers use to involve the reader in all types of literature as well as in expository writing. One method parents and students may find useful is to compare sentence and paragraph organization by critically examining a section of written prose, looking for basic elements of organization such as main thoughts with supporting details, followed by a conclusion. In a short story, the discussion might center on characterization, the setting, plot development or any other element in a fictional work.

Directions: Choose the best answer.

1. Major parts of an essay include an introduction with a topic, a series of related paragraphs, and

    a. a lot of details.
    b. no concern for the audience.
    c. illogical order.
    d. a conclusion.

2. To write a consistent essay one should first

    a. state the main purpose of the essay.
    b. choose a topic for the essay.
    c. organize topics in a logical order.
    d. locate information.

3. Types of transitions are essential in connecting ideas and maintaining order. Which word or groups of words indicate chronological order?

    a. on the right
    b. however
    c. soon
    d. finally

4. Which word or groups of words indicate the order of importance?

    a. furthermore
    b. although
    c. nearby
    d. instead

Directions: In the paragraph that follows, choose a logical transition for each numbered blank from the choices that follow.

The Sierra Nevada dictates weather patterns and climate for rather large sections of both California and Nevada. (5)_____ Pacific storms that often generate large amounts of energy, travel east across these mountains. As these fronts come in contact with the mountains, most of the precipitation falls on the western side of the Sierra. (6)_____ huge amounts of rain and snowfall on the Pacific side of the Sierra, the eastern side remains relatively dry. (7)_____, most of the moisture on the Nevada side comes during the winter.

    5.
        a. Moreover
        b. While
        c. In the first place
        d. Therefore
        e. However

    6.
        a. Moreover
        b. While
        c. In the first place
        d. Therefore
        e. However

    7.
        a. Moreover
        b. While
        c. In the first place
        d. Therefore
        e. However

8. Of the following, which technique would be most useful in writing a descriptive composition?

    a. vivid images
    b. similes and metaphors
    c. logical arguments
    d. a and c only
    e. a and b only

9. The ability to observe details is essential in descriptive writing because the writer is trying to
    a. create a picture in the mind of the reader.
    b. state an opinion for you.
    c. present information in a logical manner.
    d. persuade you to buy something.

10. Expository writing that defines, needs _____ to help the reader understand the main ideas.

    a. logical order
    b. comparisons and examples
    c. vivid images
    d. magazine articles

11. Which method is **not** used for developing an expository paragraph?

    a. illustrations
    b. defining the topic in narrow terms
    c. comparisons
    d. citing authority

12. Expository writing that explains how to do something should

    a. be convincing.
    b. be organized in a logical order.
    c. contain specific details.
    d. try to sell something.

13. Writing that is an attempt to persuade is also a type of expository writing. Which of these choices gives an important clue in writing of this type?

    a. state a conclusion
    b. give the answers
    c. state an opinion
    d. organize your evidence
    e. c and d

14. Which of these topics would be appropriate for a 500-700 word paper?

    a. soccer
    b. Hollywood films
    c. my club team's trip to Colorado Springs
    d. our country's founding fathers

15. Topics for reports or papers come from a variety of sources. Which of the following would be a good starting place to look for topics?

    a. personal experiences of your friends
    b. your own experiences
    c. articles in magazines or newspapers
    d. a and b
    e. b and c

16. A thesis is a statement of the topic and

    a. should be written as a question.
    b. is somewhat open to discussion.
    c. should be stated as an opinion.
    d. supports the introduction.

17. A series of ideas relating to your thesis statement, once listed may be organized into

    a. a conclusion.
    b. an introduction.
    c. an outline.
    d. a list of reminders.

18. Which of the following is the correct format for a bibliography listing?

    a. New Mexico's Best Ghost Towns: A Practical Guide. Varney, Philip. Flagstaff, Arizona: Northland Press, 1981.
    b. Philip Varney. New Mexico's Best Ghost Towns: A Practical Guide. Flagstaff, Arizona: Northland Press, 1981.
    c. Varney, Philip. New Mexico's Best Ghost Towns: A Practical Guide. Flagstaff, Arizona: Northland Press, 1981.

19. In writing a correct bibliography, you should **not**

    a. indent after the first line.
    b. check your punctuation.
    c. alphabetize by the author's last name.
    d. alphabetize by the title of book.

Directions: Read the following paragraph and answer the questions on organization and word choice. The questions correspond to each group of words with numbers that need to be revised.

[20] Most of my time after school is filled up with many activities like outdoor sports art classes, babysitting, and exercising. [21] Activities that occur after school prevent students from doing their very best in school. [22] I really like to play tennis in the summer. [23] My softball team practices three times each week in season and we play a tournament every month it is very much fun. [24] We ski as a family in the winter but, that doesn't take too much time because we are close to the ski lift.

20.
    a. add a colon after activities
    b. add a period after the end of the sentence
    c. eliminate the sentence altogether
    d. none of the above
    e. a and b

21.
    a. good topic sentence
    b. good topic sentence but not for this paragraph
    c. incorrect punctuation
    d. replace "very" with a descriptive word

22.
    a. add some vivid words to the sentence
    b. contains a punctuation error
    c. sentence is out of sequence
    d. no mistakes

23.
    a. replace the word 'very'
    b. sentence is out of sequence
    c. contains a run-on sentence
    d. no mistakes
    e. a and c

24.
    a. correct as is
    b. needs correct punctuation
    c. sentence is too long
    d. incorrect spelling

25. Which of the following sentences in this paragraph should be eliminated?
(With additional descriptive words and logical order this could be a good paragraph.)

      a. 20 and 24
      b. 23
      c. 21
      d. 20 and 21

Directions: In the next paragraph, pay careful attention to the structure of the paragraph, the main idea and supporting details. Choose the best answer for the questions that follow.

One thousand years ago, an amazing civilization existed in the southwestern United States. The Four Corners region, the area of present-day states of Utah, Colorado, Arizona, and New Mexico, was home to the Anasazi. Abandoning this area nearly seven hundred years ago, they left a record of their passing lifestyle. In the canyonlands and arches there is ample evidence of their existence. It is believed that these people were at one time a hunter-gatherer culture, and that they evolved, helped by the addition of new types of corn and beans, into a primarily agricultural people. To this day one can discover fragments of flint, a fine-grained type of quartz, or chert, a hardened variety of silica, near springs or cliffs. The Anasazi used both for their arrowheads. Small pieces of broken pottery called shards may also be visible to the keen eye. Along canyon walls and on rocks can be seen the carvings and paintings of animals, human figures, and designs. It is incredible that these petroglyphs and pictographs remain after more than five hundred years.

26. The topic of the paragraph is

      a. An amazing civilization existed in the Southwestern United States one thousand years ago.
      b. The Anasazi lived in parts of Utah, Colorado, Arizona, and New Mexico one thousand years ago.
      c. The Four Corners region was home to an amazing civilization.
      d. The Anasazi communicated through their drawings.

27. The sentence that begins "To this day..." is an example of this type of transition.

      a. order of importance
      b. spatial order
      c. comparison/contrast order
      d. chronological order

28. What type of context clues are given to help the reader understand flint, chert and shard?

    a. example
    b. contrast
    c. restatement
    d. none of the above

29. What evidence indicates that the Anasazi changed their lifestyle from hunting and gathering to primarily farming?

    a. a change in climate.
    b. the discovery of more water sources.
    c. their portable homes.
    d. the appearance of pottery.

30. What information could scientists gain from studying the pictographs and petrogylphs in this area?

    a. Knowledge about religion.
    b. Knowledge about animals and enemies.
    c. Patterns of movement; changes that indicate disease, drought, or famine
    d. All of the above

31. The most spectacular remains left by the Anasazi are located ten to twelve miles east of the town of Cortez in Colorado. They are the cliff dwellings of Mesa Verde, built from adobe and positioned on ledges along the cliffs. If this information was to be included as part of the previous paragraph, where would it be placed?

    a. not included at all
    b. as the topic sentence of another paragraph
    c. as a transition sentence at the end of this paragraph
    d. before the mention of pictographs and petroglyphs

Content Cluster: LITERARY ELEMENTS INCLUDING RESPONSE AND ANALYSIS

Objective: To assess the student's ability to: (1) identify purposes and characteristics of different forms of prose; (2) identify elements that relate to the plot; (3) analyze characterization as seen through a variety of views; and (4) determine contrasting points of view

> **Parent tip:** In this section a variety of written work will be examined. The selections will include works from the *Recommended Readings in Literature, Kindergarten Through Grade Eight* as part of the California State Standards. Using prose and poetry, examine as many structural types and literary terms as possible. These recommended readings offer many opportunities to become familiar with and analyze these essential literary elements.

Directions: Choose the best answer.

1. Which of the following is not an element in short stories?

    a. plot
    b. character
    c. opinion
    d. setting

2. A novella is a

    a. short non-fiction work.
    b. a short story.
    c. long non-fiction work.
    d. long short story.

3. A writer who composes a moderately brief piece of prose that attempts to convince has written

    a. an essay.
    b. a short story.
    c. a novel.
    d. a science book.

As part of the *Recommended Readings in Literature*, "The Miracle Worker" by William Gibson, and "Anne Frank: The Diary of a Young Girl", are both fine examples of age-appropriate materials. "The Miracle Worker" is a play about the struggles of Annie Sullivan and her quest to help Helen Keller learn to overcome her disabilities. "Anne Frank: The Diary of a Young Girl" is the famous true account of a young girl and her relationships with her family and others as they lived together in hiding from the Nazis in Amsterdam during the 1940's.

Directions: Here are several excerpts from both works. Read them and analyze the events that affect the plot in each through the questions that follow.

In the first accounts from "The Miracle Worker", events occur which help us understand Annie Sullivan's situation as teacher in the home of the Kellers. She is driving to the Kellers for the first time with Kate, Helen's mother and James, Helen's brother.

Kate: Helen's waiting for you too. There's been such a bustle in the house, she expects something, heaven knows what.

(Now she voices part of her doubt, not as such, but Annie understands it.)

I expected – a desiccated spinster. You're very young.
Annie [Resolutely]: Oh, you should have seen me when I left Boston. I got much older on this trip.
Kate: I mean, to teach anyone as difficult as Helen.
Annie: I mean to try. They can't put you in jail for trying!
Kate: Is it possible, even? To teach a deaf-blind child *half* of what an ordinary child learns-has that ever been done?
Annie: Half?
Kate: A tenth.
Annie [Reluctantly]: No.

(Kate's face loses its remaining hope, still appraising her youth.)

Dr. Howe did wonders, but-an ordinary child? No, never. But then I thought when I was going over his reports-

(She indicates the one in her hand.)

-he never treated them like ordinary children. More like-eggs everyone was afraid would break.

Kate [A pause]: May I ask how old you are?
Annie: Well, I'm not in my teens, you know! I'm twenty.
Kate: All of twenty.

Directions: Choose the best answer.

4. The dialogue between Annie and Kate shows that

    a. Helen was too difficult for the previous teacher, Dr. Howe.
    b. Helen was impossible to teach.
    c. Helen could not learn.
    d. Helen did not like Dr. Howe.

5. Continued references to Annie's youthfulness indicate that

    a. James thinks that she is good-looking.
    b. Kate doubts that Annie has the experience to teach Helen.
    c. In the future, Annie may encounter difficulties due to her age.
    d. a and b only
    e. b and c only

6. Which of the following accurately reflects Dr. Howe's efforts with Helen?

    a. Dr. Howe was a failure.
    b. Dr. Howe was strict with Helen.
    c. He made detailed notes.
    d. He had some success in teaching Helen.
    e. c and d

7. Annie's reference to aging on the train from Boston shows

    a. that she has a sense of humor.
    b. that she is determined.
    c. that she is confident.
    d. a and b only
    e. a, b, and c

8. Foreshadowing is indicated by

    a. a shadow behind the main character.
    b. shading in the area to give the appearance of depth.
    c. a shadow in front of the main character.
    d. hints or clues on actions to follow present events.

"Anne Frank: The Diary of a Young Girl" contains a passage in which Anne discusses her personality.

"I have one outstanding trait in my character, which must strike anyone who knows me for any length of time, and that is my knowledge of myself. I can watch myself and my actions, just like an outsider. The Anne of every day I can face entirely without prejudice, without making excuses for her and watch what's good and what's bad about her. This "self-consciousness" haunts me, and every time I open my mouth I know as soon as I've spoken whether "that ought to have been different" or "that was right as it was." There are so many things about myself that I condemn; I couldn't begin to name them all"...

"In addition to this, I have lots of courage, I always feel so strong and as if I can bear a great deal, I feel so free and so young! I was glad when I first realized it, because I don't think I shall easily bow down before the blows that inevitably come to everyone."

9. Anne describes her personality as having "self-consciousness". Which of the following is **not** accurate about Anne's view of herself?

    a. Anne is aware of her good qualities.
    b. Anne is self-centered.
    c. Anne is aware that at times she may not say the right thing.
    d. Anne has self-confidence.

10. Another quality that Anne possesses is that of courage. She knows that in the future,

    a. she will have an easy time making decisions.
    b. her mother and father will always help her with decisions.
    c. there will be difficult decisions to be made.
    d. decisions will be made for her.

11. In general, Anne would describe the way in which she looks at herself as

    a. realistic.
    b. one-sided.
    c. incompatible.
    d. lacking ingenuity.

Within the context of World War II and the Amsterdam apartment where Anne and her family were hiding, she made these observations on the differences between generations:

"Is it true then that grown-ups have a more difficult time here than we do? No. I know it isn't. Older people have formed their opinions about everything, and don't waver before they act. It's twice as hard for us young ones to hold our ground, and maintain our opinions, in a time when all ideals are being shattered and destroyed, when people are showing their worst side, and do not know whether to believe in truth and right and God."

12. For Anne, youth is a more difficult time that adulthood because

    a. youth has all the answers.
    b. adults are steadfast in their opinions.
    c. youth has formed their opinions.
    d. both groups do not understand each other.

13. According to Anne, why is it difficult for youth to shape their opinions?

    a. Youth does not have experience with which to form ideas.
    b. Problems of youth have easy solutions.
    c. Youth has fresh ideas.
    d. In the world, people are destroying ideas, dreams, and hope.

14. Because the older generations are devastating society and its ideals, it is

    a. easy for youth to become discontented.
    b. easy for youth to discover answers to problems.
    c. hard to understand youth.
    d. easy to rely on hope.

Directions: Read the following passages and choose the best answer to the questions that follow.

There was never a more exciting time than the Fourth of July in Estelline, South Dakota. It was a celebration for all ages including a parade, ceremonies, picnics, ball games, a grandstand show with, of course, fireworks. Because my grandparents lived there, I always looked forward to this time as a chance to visit them. In addition, fireworks were illegal in Minnesota where I lived. I would save my hard earned money from a variety of lawn mowing jobs, add this to my allowance and hope I had enough to buy as many firecrackers as I possibly could afford.

On this particular Fourth, which promised to be the best of all, there was an evening show at the grandstand of the dirt racetrack at the west end of town. The racing in the afternoon had long since ended. Preparations had transformed the track into a stage complete with lights and sound system.

As he remembers, there were at least two large grandstand sections built mostly of wood. His grandparents were seated on the very front row in front of the stage. He was on the top row of the bleachers, probably twenty-five rows up, in the far west corner leaning against the railing which helped to support the structure. On his right was a narrow entrance to the front of the grandstand, with an identical grandstand section beyond that.

The evening began with local acts of comedians and singing groups. Stands were packed with people and more came in after the entertainment had started. Suddenly, with the program barely underway, the musical sound was interrupted by the sound of splitting wood, gasps and shouts from the crowd as the entire structure on which he was standing gave way. He grabbed the railing and rode the collapsing bleacher section as it fell, not straight down but toward the right, stopping as it came into contact with the next section of bleachers. There was a pause as the music stopped, and people began helping those hurt. He searched for his grandparents and found them at the foot of the stands. Grandfather was all right but grandmother had some minor internal injuries. He never forgot that Fourth of July in Estelline.

15. In this example, there is a change in the narration from

    a. third person to first person.
    b. second person to first person.
    c. second person to third person.
    d. first person to third person.

16. In any first person narration, a writer

    a. tells the story without feeling.
    b. tells the story as if she participated in the action.
    c. tells the story as if he was observing the action.
    d. tells the story adding conflict.

17. In any third person narration, a writer

   a. tells the story with feeling.
   b. tells the story as if she participated in the action.
   c. tells the story as if he was observing the action.
   d. tells the story adding resolution.

18. In the previous passage, the author

   a. witnesses the grandstand collapse.
   b. tells the story of the grandstand collapsing.
   c. pretends to observe the collapse of the bleachers.
   d. participates in the grandstand collapse.

19. In the previous passage, the author

   a. regrets leaving Minnesota for the Fourth of July.
   b. looks forward to visiting Estelline for the Fourth of July.
   c. never returned to Estelline after the bleacher collapsed.
   d. wants to move to South Dakota.

20. Which of the following descriptions is **not** an example of literary setting?

   a. white puffy clouds drifting lazily across the sky
   b. the close-knit community of look-alike homes
   c. it was a time of Model A automobiles and wide-brimmed hats
   d. the five-story gray tenement building

21. In this short poem, describe the literary element used.

   Silently, at first, above the discordant hum,
   the unmistakable call of wild geese heading south.

   a. characterization
   b. setting
   c. personification
   d. imagery

Content Cluster: WRITING APPLICATIONS

Objective: To assess student's knowledge of: (1) fictional or autobiographical narratives; (2) literary interpretation; (3) written research reports; (4) persuasive writing; and (5) summaries of informational reading.

Parent Tip: The California State Standard asks seventh grade students to write "narrative, expository, persuasive, and descriptive" essays of 500 – 700 words. In assisting with this task, it is important to use the suggestions given in the strategies section as well as the standard conventions of proper grammar. As was mentioned earlier, daily writing in a journal, or writing stories are valuable ways in which to improve writing skills. In addition to reading and learning a new word each day, writing each will help you improve a skill necessary for life.

Directions: Choose the correct answer.

1. A fictional narrative text usually contains a standard plot line.
   Which of the following develops a plot in correct order?

   a. beginning, rising action, climax, conflict, and resolution
   b. rising action, climax, beginning, conflict, and resolution
   c. beginning, conflict, climax, rising action, and resolution
   d. beginning, conflict, rising action, climax, and resolution

2. Character development is essential in fiction writing. The main character is multi-faceted, or possessing several traits, and is the most important person in the story. A direct characterization would be one in which

   a. the writer allows the reader to form her own ideas about the character.
   b. the writer uses actions or speech to describe the character.
   c. the writer states the qualities of the character.
   d. the writer allows other characters in the story to describe the character.

3. Another way in which an author may develop a character is through indirect characterization. In this method, the writer

   a. uses actions or speech in describing the character.
   b. states the personality of the character.
   c. describes the character through other characters in the story.
   d. a and b
   e. b and c

4. A minor character takes part in the action but

    a. has a key role in the outcome.
    b. is usually not the center of attention.
    c. relies on the main character for support.
    d. is always behind the main character.

5. Setting provides the reader with a context for the action. In addition to time and place, which of the following is important to the setting?

    a. types of transportation
    b. community
    c. time of year
    d. language dialects
    e. all of the above

6. The narrator can involve the characters in the action of the story by the use of

    a. hand or arm gestures.
    b. facial expressions.
    c. various types of movements.
    d. a, b, and c
    e. neither a, b, nor c

In the following excerpt from "The Miracle Worker," the combination of both dialogue and stage direction create the basic situation and set the tone for the story to unfold.

The doctor has just left and Kate Keller is standing over the crib.

KATE: Hush. Don't you cry now, you've been trouble enough. Call it acute congestion, indeed, I don't see what's so cute about a congestion, just because it' yours. We'll have your father run an editorial in his paper, the wonders of modern medicine…
Men, men and their battle scars, we women will have to-

(But she breaks off, puzzled, moves her finger before the baby's eyes.)

Will have to – Helen?

(Now she moves her hand, quickly.)

Helen.

(She snaps her fingers at the baby's eyes twice, and her hand falters; after a moment she calls out, loudly.)

Captain. Captain, will you come-

(But she stares at the baby, and her next call is directly at her ears.)

Captain!

(And now, still staring, KATE screams. KELLER in the yard hears it, and runs with the lamp back to the house. KATE screams again, her look intent on the baby and terrible. KELLER hurries in and up.)

KELLER: Katie? What's wrong?

KATE: Look.

7. This example illustrates strategies that may be used to

    a.   create the setting.
    b.   develop the minor character.
    c.   build suspense.
    d.   a and b
    e.   a and c

8. In this example, the uncertainty of the outcome is introduced by

    a.   stage directions that show the actors where to move on the stage.
    b.   the distance between Kate Keller and her husband.
    c.   the dialogue between Kate and her husband.
    d.   stage directions that show emotion and a lapse of time.

9. In responding to literature, a thorough examination of characters and their traits is one way to develop insightful interpretations. Which one of the following would **not** be essential in this regard?

    a.   understanding which character is a stereotype
    b.   a listing of each characters traits
    c.   to list the names of the characters in alphabetical order
    d.   motivation and development of the characters
    e.   to compare and contrast two or more characters

10. The setting is the time and place of the story, and provides a backdrop for the action. When interpreting images or ideas, which of the following would be critical?

    a. general knowledge of regions in the United States or the world
    b. clues to the passage or change of time
    c. the color of the oak leaves in the autumn
    d. b and c
    e. a and b

11. A theme may be either stated or implied. Which of the following would **not** be a method a writer would use to tell the story?

    a. stated directly by the narrator
    b. stated through a character
    c. having a character suggest the theme
    d. writing it at the beginning of the story

12. Some useful ways to respond to questions regarding the main ideas or themes of stories are to paraphrase the main ideas, to list the main ideas, and to

    a. observe the main character and how the character changes.
    b. ask why characters behave in certain ways.
    c. project possible variations and their effect on the theme.
    d. organize them into an outline

13. A key element in any literary work is conflict. Conflict causes action and is categorized into two main types:

    a. man against man
    b. man against nature
    c. man against himself
    d. external and internal
    e. external and implied

14. In examining literature, the common elements of _____, fit together. Find as many details relating to each element as you can. The more evidence you can acquire, the more accurate your interpretation will be.

    a. character, plot, harmony, and nature
    b. character, setting, harmony, and theme
    c. character, setting, plot, and theme
    d. plot, character, theme, and design

Note: Curriculum standards usually require the organization and writing of research reports. Report topic selection is vital in the overall process. If a general topic is the area of sports, it is important to use strategies to narrow this area because it is too broad for a two to four page report. The following questions focus on this standard.

15. Sports are an area that requires reduction. What are some possible ways this topic may be narrowed?

    a.   choose a particular sport
    b.   choose a particular level
    c.   choose a certain country
    d.   choose a new topic

16. The topic has been narrowed to football, but it still is too general. What could be done to make the topic more manageable?

    a.   pick a certain level of football to research
    b.   compare football and basketball
    c.   decide to research the development of protective equipment
    d.   a and b
    e.   a and c

17. Professional football reduces the range even more, however it is still too broad. Which of these areas would be an appropriate topic for a paper of this length?

    a.   the history of the Super Bowl
    b.   the greatest players of all time
    c.   the greatest quarterbacks of all time
    d.   the benefits and dangers of professional preseason football games

18. Some questions that could be asked about professional preseason football games are:

    a.   What is the history of preseason games?
    b.   What are the benefits of preseason games?
    c.   What are the risks of preseason games?
    d.   What is the status currently of preseason games?
    e.   all of the above

19. Using questions as a beginning point, begin the task of locating information by

    a.   reading from a variety of sources.
    b.   recording relevant sources as bibliographies.
    c.   writing notes.
    d.   a and b
    e.   b and c

20. Which of the following would be least likely to contain relevant information on professional preseason football games?

    a.   an encyclopedia
    b.   a newspaper
    c.   a television show
    d.   a magazine
    e.   a book

21. After notes have been taken, the next task is to

    a.   make an outline
    b.   evaluate information, looking for incomplete sections
    c.   determine facts from opinions
    d.   all of the above
    e.   b and c only

22. Next is the writing. It is crucial to

    a.   state ideas in your own words.
    b.   have someone write for you.
    c.   document sources by giving appropriate credit to original authors.
    d.   a and c
    e.   a and b

23. There are a variety of methods that can be used to document original material, including quotes and footnotes. Which of the following is a correct footnote format?

    a.   *Dylan Thomas*, Paul Ferris, (Dial Press: New York, 1977) p. 288.
    b.   Ferris, Paul, *Thomas Dylan*, (Dial Press: New York, 1977), p. 288.
    c.   Paul Ferris, *Dylan Thomas* (New York: Dial Press,1977), p. 288.
    d.   Paul Ferris, *Dylan Thomas* (New York: Dial Press, 1977), p. 288

24. Persuasive writing is designed to

    a.   state an opinion with little or no justification at all.
    b.   offer the best solution to a difficulty.
    c.   convince the reader to adopt a particular course of action.
    d.   inform the public.

Directions: Read the paragraph and answer the following questions.

In light of the rising cost of gasoline and a worldwide oil shortage, an idea that merits serious consideration is the fuel-efficient vehicle. Gasoline costs have increased dramatically during the past few years. Meanwhile, the surplus of oil throughout the world is reported to be falling at an alarming rate. Instead of reducing our gasoline consumption, the American public is obsessed with sport utility vehicles, other fuel wasting automobiles and their horrible miles per gallon ratings.

There are a variety of methods that have helped in reducing emissions. Most cars have computers, which help regulate the fuel mixture through injector systems. Since the late 1970's, catalytic converters have assisted exhaust systems change harmful pollutants into water, oxygen, and carbon dioxide. Finally, various types of gasoline additives have been used to decrease pollution, including adding oxygen compounds to make the gasoline burn cleaner. This has been helpful in reducing global warming.

As gasoline prices steadily increase to a point where many people can't afford it, many oil producing countries have either cut production or returned to earlier levels. The discovery of significant oil producing fields has diminished as we consume this finite resource. While presidents and energy secretaries fly all over the world to attend meetings on the significance of the situation, the people pay up to two dollars per gallon for gas. We really need fuel-efficient vehicles.

25. In the brief introduction, the most important point the writer makes is that

    a. the surplus of oil throughout the world is falling.
    b. the time for fuel-efficient vehicles has come.
    c. America really likes sport utility vehicles.
    d. gas prices have increased.

26. The main idea of the second paragraph is that

    a. there are many types of cars.
    b. there are many systems in place to help reduce emissions.
    c. gasoline additives have been used to reduce pollution.
    d. there are systems which have reduced global warming.

27. The second paragraph

    a. discussed types of vehicles.
    b. supports the author's views on low-emission vehicles.
    c. does not justify or support the author's proposition.
    d. sounds good and has some valuable information.

28. What other kinds of information are necessary to support the author's point of view?

    a. information on alternative fuel vehicles such as hybrids, EV's, hydrogen and natural gas vehicles
    b. statistics on oil consumption
    c. information on global warming
    d. a and b
    e. a and c

29. What would sport utility vehicle owners say to the argument for fuel-efficient vehicles?

    a. Sport utility vehicles are more practical.
    b. Sport utility vehicles look good and have power.
    c. Alternative fuel vehicles look strange.
    d. all of the above

30. In order to address reader concerns the writer would anticipate the arguments from auto manufacturers such as:

    a. Alternative fuel vehicles don't sell.
    b. We are making sport utility vehicles that are extremely fuel-efficient.
    c. Our customers are buying sport utility vehicles.
    d. a and b
    e. a and c

In summarizing informational reading material, it is beneficial to list main points and supporting details. In addition, it may help to reflect on any hidden ideas, or underlying meanings that are implied or suggested. Thus the reader is using logical thought to analyze the material. These passages that are excerpted from the *Magna Carta*, are followed by questions dealing with both factual material and implied ideas.

No constable or other bailiff of ours [i.e., the king] shall take anyone's grain or other chattels without immediately paying for them in money, unless he is able to obtain a postponement at the good will of the seller.

No sheriff or bailiff of ours [i.e., the king] or any one else, shall take horses or wagons of any free man, for carrying purposes, except on the permission of that free man.

bailiff – a law officer
chattels – personal property

31. The main ideas of these two brief sections of the *Magna Carta* are:

    a. No law officer may arrest anyone.
    b. No law officer can take personal property from anyone without paying for it.
    c. No law officer can take horses or wagons to use for carrying purposes, except by permission.
    d. a and b
    e. b and c

32. Ideas that are not stated but are implied in the sections are:

    a. There is an official law of the land.
    b. The king cannot take horses.
    c. A bailiff may pay for the use of grain by trading other items.
    d. The king is not above the law; he must follow the rule of law.

No free man shall be taken, or imprisoned, or banished, or in any way injured, nor will we go upon him, nor send upon him, except by the legal judgment of his peers, or by the law of the land.

33. The main point in this part of the *Magna Carta* is:

    a. No free man may be imprisoned or banished.
    b. No free man may be jailed or banished except by a jury of his peers, or by the law of the land.
    c. No free man may be imprisoned or banished except by the king.
    d. The king may seize people to imprison them.

34. Implied ideas in this section of the *Magna Carta* are:

    a. The document sets forth the idea of trial by peers or a jury.
    b. Many nobles worked as bailiffs and did not need to obey the law.
    c. People had rights the king could not take away.
    d. a and b
    e. a and c

Content Cluster: SENTENCE STRUCTURE AND GRAMMAR ANALYSIS

Objectives: To evaluate and aid the student's understanding of: (1) the correct placement of adjectives, adverbs, and prepositional phrases used as modifiers; (2) the correct use of infinitives and participles; (3) the relationship between pronouns and antecedents; (4) punctuation; (5) capitalization; and (5) spelling.

Parent Tip: Success in understanding and using modifiers assumes students can identify basic parts of speech as well as basic sentence structure. A simple review of nouns, verbs, and adjectives could be a starting point as you begin this section.

Directions: Identify the noun modifier(s).

Example: Mr. Jones was most often a happy man.
   a. Mr. Jones
   b. happy
   c. man
   d. often

The correct answer is "b." Happy is a descriptive adjective modifying the noun 'man'.

1. The writer was unable to type with consistency.

   a. the
   b. writer
   c. unable
   d. type

2. Volleyball players filled the gym.

   a. volleyball
   b. players
   c. gym
   d. filled

3. Susy jumped as the annoying alarm clock went off at 6:00.

    a. jumped
    b. Susy
    c. alarm clock
    d. annoying

4. As they drove on the parkway, autumn colors radiated from the hillsides.

    a. hillsides
    b. they
    c. autumn
    d. parkway
    e. color

Directions: Identify the verb modifiers.

Example: The English class moved quickly.

    a. English
    b. moved
    c. quickly
    d. class

The correct answer is "c". Quickly describes the manner in which the class moved.

5. An ambulance siren wailed loudly.

    a. loudly
    b. ambulance
    c. An
    d. wailed

6. On the top of the pine tree, an owl occasionally hooted.

    a. pine tree
    b. occasionally
    c. hooted
    d. owl

7. They confidently expected to return with a limit of good-sized tuna.

    a. size
    b. confidently
    c. good
    d. expected

8. The movie stars were extravagantly dressed for the gala event.

    a. movie
    b. dressed
    c. event
    d. extravagantly

9. Rapidly gliding, the surfer shot through the barrel.

    a. Rapidly
    b. through
    c. barrel
    d. gliding

NOTE: Adverbs may also modify adjectives as in; She was a <u>very</u> happy girl. They may also modify other adverbs as in; The egg was <u>too</u> soft.

Parent Tip: Prepositions add dimension to sentences. Prepositional phrases such as, through the decades, and over the mountains, may serve as modifiers of nouns or adjectives. Common prepositions include words like; of, about, across, into, and around.

Example: After breakfast, the boys relaxed in the shade while waiting to swim across the lake.

*Prepositions	Prepositional Phrases
in	in the shade
across	across the lake

"After" and "to" are prepositions also, but are not part of prepositional phrases in the sentence.

Directions: Identify the prepositions in the following sentences.

10. Few young people lived in the small town.

    a. Few
    b. lived
    c. in
    d. small

11. Betty figured she could call in to the radio station for tickets.

    a. she
    b. to
    c. for
    d. b and c

12. Sometimes freeway noise disturbs the class.

    a. sometimes
    b. noise
    c. disturbs
    d. none of the above

13. The children traveled by airplane to visit relatives.

    a. visit
    b. by
    c. to
    d. b and c

Directions: Identify the prepositional phrases in the following sentences.

14. Across the river, the traffic was backed up for miles.

    a. up for miles
    b. across the river
    c. backed up
    d. traffic was backed up

15 .The spotted dog, running quickly, disappeared behind the store.

    a. the spotted dog
    b. behind the store
    c. running quickly
    d. disappeared

16. You will not be able to vote outside the school.

    a. not be able
    b. You will not
    c. outside the school
    d. to vote

17. Steady pack mules deliver mail to the bottom of the Grand Canyon.

   a. Steady pack mules
   b. to the bottom
   c. of the Grand Canyon
   d. a and b
   e. b and c

Objective: Students will understand correct use of infinitives and participles.

> **Parent Tip:** Infinitives are verbs, which are preceded by the word "to". The phrase may be used as a noun, an adjective, or an adverb.

Examples: In these examples, <u>to design</u> is the infinitive, and, <u>to design computer software</u> is the infinitive phrase.

   1. To design computer software is David's dream. (phrase used as a noun)
   2. The best place to design computer software is in the computer lab. (phrase used as an adjective)
   3. David learned to design computer software. (phrase used an adverb)

Directions: Identify the infinitive phrases.

18. The neighbors gave Julie twenty dollars to baby-sit their toddler.

   a. gave Julie twenty dollars
   b. to baby sit
   c. to baby sit their toddler
   d. The neighbors

19. James is trying to learn Spanish and French.

   a. is trying
   b. to learn Spanish and French
   c. to learn
   d. none of the above

20. Mrs. Graham's class used the quadratic equation to solve math problems.

   a. to solve math problems
   b. used the quadratic equation
   c. math problems
   d. b and c

21. Dr. Moore attempted to explain and analyze his theory.

    a. attempted to explain
    b. to explain
    c. his theory
    d. to explain and analyze his theory

22. In traveling across Texas, the family saw the flashing lights of a low-flying airplane.

    a. saw the flashing lights
    b. of a low-flying airplane
    c. in traveling across Texas
    d. the flashing lights
    e. none of the above

Parent tip: A participle is a verb form that usually functions as an adjective.

Directions: Choose the participle.

23. The freezing rain caused numerous accidents on the freeway.

    a. numerous
    b. freezing
    c. rain
    d. freeway

24. Having won the relay, the track team celebrated.

    a. track
    b. celebrated
    c. relay
    d. Having

25. Swimming rapidly, the fish snatched the minnow.

    a. rapidly
    b. Swimming
    c. snatched
    d. minnow

26. A blue heron, emerging from the water, soared gracefully.

   a. blue
   b. heron
   c. emerging
   d. water
   e. soared

Objective: Students will understand the relationship between pronouns and antecedents.

Parent tip: The pronoun and the antecedent (the word to which the pronoun refers) must agree in number, gender, and person.

Example: The girls were able to complete *their* assignments before the due date. In this case, the pronoun 'their' refers to girls. It agrees in gender and number as well as person.

Directions: In the following sentences if the italicized pronoun is not in agreement with its antecedent, choose the correct one.

27. The staff invites you to join *him* for a specially prepared luncheon.

   a. them
   b. us
   c. she
   d. correct as is

28. Each boy should submit *her* entry by Friday.

   a. their
   b. they're
   c. his
   d. correct as is

29. If anyone knows the name of that song, *he* should call the radio station for a prize.

   a. she
   b. they
   c. me
   d. correct as is

30. The manufacturers decided to increase *they're* auto prices for the New Year.

    a. them
    b. her
    c. their
    d. correct as is

31. Anderson Middle School lost part of *there* roof in the heavy wind storm.

    a. its
    b. it's
    c. their
    d. correct as is

32. While we were rehearsing, everyone forgot *his* lines.

    a. their
    b. they're
    c. her
    d. correct as is

Objective: Identify the proper standard English pronoun.

Directions: Choose the best answer.

33. The Smiths got their cat from the same pet store as _____.

    a. we
    b. us
    c. them
    d. her

34. No one believed that Carl would work longer than _____, but Carl worked five more hours than Joe.

    a. he
    b. him
    c. us
    d. them

35. Dan Herder is the tennis instructor _____ I described in my memo to you this morning.

    a. what
    b. who
    c. when
    d. whom

36. I know _____ you should ask to the dance, but I'm not telling.

    a. whom
    b. who
    c. what
    d. why

37. Someone had left _____ ice cream melting on the sidewalk and that is what attracted the ants.

    a. there
    b. his
    c. their
    d. her

38. My father's company has a great incentive program for _____ employees.

    a. its
    b. his
    c. their
    d. them

39. Sally and _____ took turns doing the dishes.

    a. me
    b. myself
    c. her
    d. I

40. It would be reasonable for someone in the skateboard accident to blame _____.

    a. himself
    b. hisself
    c. yourself
    d. themself

Objective: To use basic parts of speech correctly.

Directions: In the sentences that follow, identify the italicized words.

41. The winter storm moved steadily through the *Rocky Mountains.*

    a. common noun
    b. proper noun
    c. verb
    d. adverb

42. Some authors write books based upon *imaginary* stories.

    a. verb
    b. adverb
    c. adjective
    d. common noun

43. I recommend making an appointment *at* your earliest convenience.

    a. preposition
    b. noun
    c. verb
    d. adjective

44. The customer service department has been helpful in offering *assistance.*

    a. noun
    b. adjective
    c. verb
    d. none of the above

45. Mrs. Paul *traveled* to Chicago from New Orleans.

    a. noun
    b. adverb
    c. adjective
    d. verb

46. In some states, owners of *large* or fancy automobiles must pay a luxury tax on these vehicles.

    a. noun
    b. adjective
    c. verb
    d. none of the above

47. Jenny Dilberg *and* her daughter were playing tennis.

    a. noun
    b. verb
    c. adjective
    d. none of the above

48. The dogs played *dangerously* close to the street.

    a. noun
    b. verb
    c. adverb
    d. conjunction

49. *Too* many mosquitoes forced the dinner party guests indoors.

    a. adjective
    b. adverb
    c. verb
    d. none of the above

50. Several beaches *were* closed due to the high bacteria levels.

    a. adjective
    b. noun
    c. adverb
    d. none of the above

Objective: To identify the correct punctuation.

Directions: In the following four groups of sentences, choose the sentence with correct punctuation.

51.
    a. The pres. of the sports network resigned.
    b. She is a member of the national team however she is injured.
    c. The club team will travel to Orlando, Florida.
    d. Basketball fundamentals of ball handling passing, and shooting will be taught.

52.
    a. The Chinese inventions were incomparable printing and gunpowder had a great impact on many civilizations.
    b. The Chinese inventions were incomparable; printing and gunpowder had a great impact on many civilizations.
    c. The Chinese inventions were incomparable, printing, and gunpowder had a great impact on many civilizations.
    d. The Chinese inventions were incomparable. Printing and gunpowder had a great impact on many civilizations.

53.
    a. Many students have the ability to read well; others benefit by additional instruction.
    b. Many students have the ability to read well, others benefit by additional instruction.
    c. Many students, have the ability to read well. Others benefit by additional instruction.
    d. While many students have the ability to read well. Others benefit by additional instruction.

54.
    a. Talking on cell phones while driving is legal. However many people think its dangerous.
    b. Many people think talking on cell phones, while driving is dangerous. But it is legal.
    c. While talking on cell phones and driving. Many people think it's dangerous.
    d. Talking on cell phones while driving is legal; however, many people think it's dangerous.

55. Which of the following illustrates the correct usage of brackets?

    a. Because this project is worth eighty percent of your grade (and we've discussed cooperation [although this can be a problem]), it is important to complete it on time.
    b. Because this project is worth eighty percent of your grade, and we've discussed cooperation ([although this can be a problem] it is important to complete it on time).
    c. Because (this project is worth [eighty percent] of your grade) and we've discussed cooperation; although this can be a problem, it is important to complete it on time.
    d. none of the above

56. Which of the following is **not** a correct use of the hyphen?

    a. between some prefixes and roots eg. re-lease
    b. some compounds eg. governor-elect
    c. with compound numbers between 21 and 99
    d. with dialogue eg. She said - It was great!
    e. with some modifiers eg. high-grade ore

Directions: Which of the following uses quotations correctly?

57.
    a. My sister said, " that she was bitten by a bee."
    b. "My sister said, that she was bitten by a bee."
    c. My sister said, "That she was bitten by a bee."
    d. not a quote

58.
    a. "Some species of animals," said the biologist, "Are endangered."
    b. "Some species of animals," said the biologist, are endangered.
    c. "Some species of animals," said the biologist, "are endangered."
    d. not a quote

59.
    a. "I really like volleyball now." said Catherine, "Maybe I'll play in high school."
    b. "I really like volleyball now," said Catherine. "Maybe I'll play in high school."
    c. "I really like volleyball now said Catherine." Maybe I'll play in high school.
    d. not a quote

60.
    a. The professor asked, "How many of you have read the works of Shakespeare"?
    b. The professor asked. "How many of you have read the works of Shakespeare?"
    c. The professor asked, "How many of you have read the works of Shakespeare?"
    d. not a quote

61.
   a. James stated, "That he had finished the project on time."
   b. Maria exclaimed, "I love that Steinbeck story!"
   c. "Let's get a smoothie," suggested Erin. I'll even buy!"
   d. "It's time to move toward a solution for the much debated problem."

Directions: Choose the correctly capitalized sentence or the best answer.

62.
   a. mrs. Jones decided that it would be wonderful to visit Yosemite national park.
   b. Mrs. jones decided that it would be wonderful to visit Yosemite National park.
   c. Mrs. Jones decided that it would be wonderful to visit Yosemite National park.
   d. Mrs. Jones decided that it would be wonderful to visit Yosemite National Park.

63. Which of the following are **not** capitalized?

   a. proper names of persons
   b. common nouns
   c. names of religions
   d. names of nationalities

64.
   a. Johnson hall will be the site of the pythagorean mathematicians club meeting.
   b. Johnson hall will be the site of the Pythagorean Mathematicians Club Meeting.
   c. Johnson Hall will be the site of the Pythagorean Mathematicians Club meeting.
   d. Johnson Hall will be the site of the Pythagorean mathematicians club meeting.

65.
   a. the Period of the Reformation was characterized by protests against the Catholic Church.
   b. The period of the reformation was characterized by protests against the Catholic Church.
   c. The Period of the Reformation was characterized by protests against the catholic church.
   d. The period of the Reformation was characterized by protests against the Catholic church.

66. Points on the compass are usually not capitalized unless they

   a. appear at right angles on the map.
   b. indicate areas of the country or world.
   c. show directions.
   d. are opposite in direction.

67.
   a. Economies in many countries of the far east like China, Indonesia, and South Korea are growing.
   b. Economies in many countries of the Far East like China, Indonesia, and South Korea are growing.
   c. Economies in many countries of the far East like china, Indonesia, and south korea are growing.
   d. Economies in many countries of the far east like China, Indonesia, and South Korea are growing.

68.
   a. His norwegian ancestors had moved from fillmore county in Minnesota to hamlin county in south Dakota
   b. His Norwegian ancestors had moved from Fillmore county in Minnesota to Hamlin county in South Dakota.
   c. His Norwegian ancestors had moved from Fillmore County in Minnesota to Hamlin County in South Dakota.
   d. His norwegian ancestors had moved from Fillmore County in Minnesota to Hamlin County in South Dakota.

69.
   a. Five girl scouts were missing on a hike in rocky mountain national park.
   b. Five Girl Scouts were missing on a hike in Rocky Mountain national park.
   c. Five Girl Scouts were missing on a hike in Rocky Mountain National Park.
   d. Five girl scouts were missing on a hike in Rocky Mountain National Park.

Directions: In the next several sentences, choose from the answers, the words that should be capitalized.

Example: the green bay packers will play an exhibition game in san diego

The, Green Bay, Packers, and San Diego should be capitalized

70. jack london's famous short story, "To build a Fire" takes place in the yukon winter.

   a. Jack London's, and Yukon should be capitalized
   b. Jack London's, Build, and Yukon should be capitalized
   c. Jack, Short Story, and Yukon should be capitalized
   d. Jack London's, Build, Yukon, and Winter should be capitalized

71. mt. whitney, california's tallest mountain, is located in the sierra nevada.

   a. Mt. Whitney, California's, and Nevada should be capitalized
   b. Whitney, California's, and Nevada should be capitalized
   c. California's, Mountain, and Sierra Nevada should be capitalized
   d. Mt. Whitney, California's and Sierra Nevada should be capitalized

72. william sidney porter or o. henry as he was known, wrote stories about ordinary people such as the "the ransom of red chief."

   a. William Sidney Porter, O. Henry, and The Ransom of Red Chief should be capitalized
   b. William Sidney Porter, and Ransom of Red Chief should be capitalized
   c. William Sidney Porter, Henry, and The Ransom of Red Chief should be capitalized
   d. Correct as it is

In each group of words, choose the word that is spelled <u>incorrectly</u>.

	a.	b.	c.	d.
73.	existence	acceptence	subsistence	independence
74.	ninety	fidelity	criticize	priviledge
75.	faxsimile	facile	fatigue	fallacious
76.	precedent	precidential	personable	pedigree
77.	sedition	scrumptious	reconciliacion	interruption
78.	knowledge	imaginary	favorite	judgement
79.	hier	magisterial	excommunication	homage
80.	inquisition	currency	seculer	isolation
81.	villain	temprament	occasion	ninety
82.	accumulate	prudence	competent	reconoiter
83.	reciprocle	inaudible	polytheism	anthology
84.	adherence	roll model	capitulate	tedious
85.	paucity	frivolous	congenial	pugnatious

In each group of words, choose the word that is spelled <u>correctly</u>.

	a.	b.	c.	d.
86.	detestible	sensorship	inarticulate	idiosincracy
87.	entymology	illiterate	fasinating	cronologicle
88.	exaggereted	bibliographys	poisonous	amplefyed
89.	obedient	charetible	progidy	dignateries
90.	desparacion	manefistation	indigenous	comisserate
91.	ostensabley	crucialfixion	concievible	ironically
92.	preavalant	concuistador	philosophe	alaince
93.	altiplano	bulliyon	fuetalism	Daoism
94.	sucesion	acheivments	tolarance	ethnolinguistics
95.	caliphe	satillete	accurately	acupuncture
96.	spoonirism	justify	permiate	iniptitute
97.	interpretation	creamation	burahcracy	infidle
98.	predistenation	mercantilism	parlament	courter
99.	Buddhism	sedintery	heiroglyf	responsabelity
100.	indiscret	increjulous	iridyscent	blathering

MATH

Content Cluster – NUMBER SENSE (Scientific Notation)

Objective: Students will read, write and compare rational numbers in scientific notation (positive and negative powers of 10).

> **Parent Tip:** Scientific notation is a standard number (every day number) expressed in the form of **one** digit (1-9), with all other digits after a decimal point, times 10 to a power.
>
> Example: $3,000 = 3 \times 10^3$ $14,800 = 1.48 \times 10^4$
>
> $3,400 = 3.4 \times 10^3$ $37,649 = 3.7649 \times 10^4$
>
> When the exponent is negative, the standard number will be a decimal fraction.
>
> Example: $0.00432 = 4.32 \times 10^{-3}$ $0.0000836 = 8.36 \times 10^{-5}$

10/20

Read the following numbers:

1. 4×10^4

    a. forty thousand
    b. four thousand
    c. four hundred
    d. forty

2. 8.6×10^5

    a. eight hundred sixty
    b. eight thousand, six hundred
    c. eighty-six thousand
    d. eight hundred sixty thousand

3. 3.2×10^2

    a. thirty-two
    b. three hundred twenty
    c. three thousand, two hundred
    d. thirty-two thousand

4. 2×10^6

    a. two billion
    b. two million
    c. two thousand
    d. two hundred

5. 7.3×10^{-1}

    a. seventy-three ten-thousandths
    b. seventy-three thousandths
    c. seventy-three hundredths
    d. seven and three tenths

6. 1.2×10^{-3}

    a. twelve hundredths
    b. twelve thousandths
    c. twelve ten-thousandths
    d. twelve hundred-thousandths

CONTENT CLUSTER – Number Sense (Scientific Notation)

7. 5.9×10^{-2}

    a. fifty-nine
    b. five and nine tenths
    c. fifty-nine hundredths
    d. fifty-nine thousandths

8. 6×10^{-6}

    a. six millionths
    b. six hundred-thousandths
    c. six ten-thousandths
    d. six thousandths

Write the following numbers in scientific notation:

9. 8,800

    a. 8.8×10^{1}
    b. 8.8×10^{2}
    c. 8.8×10^{3}
    d. 8.8×10^{4}

10. 6,200,000

    a. 6.2×10^{3}
    b. 6.2×10^{4}
    c. 6.2×10^{5}
    d. 6.2×10^{6}

11. 0.035

    a. 3.5×10^{-2}
    b. 3.5×10^{-3}
    c. 3.5×10^{-4}
    d. 3.5×10^{-5}

12. 0.0007

    a. 7×10^{-4}
    b. 7×10^{-3}
    c. 7×10^{-2}
    d. 7×10^{-1}

13. 38

    a. 3.8×10^{0}
    b. 3.8×10^{1}
    c. 3.8×10^{2}
    d. 3.8×10^{3}

14. 0.2

    a. 2×10^{0}
    b. 2×10^{-1}
    c. 2×10^{-2}
    d. 2×10^{-3}

CONTENT CLUSTER – Number Sense (Scientific Notation)

Parent Tip: Start by looking at the powers of ten – 1) if the exponent is **positive**, the smaller the exponent, the smaller the number – 2) if the exponent is **negative**, the larger the exponent, the smaller the number and – 3) if all the exponents are the **same**, look at the numbers and order them by size.

Examples: Ordering from least to greatest:

All positive -	**All negative -**	**All the same -**
$3\times10^3, 6\times10^1, 9\times10^7$	$9\times10^{-3}, 6\times10^{-1}, 3\times10^{-7}$	$3\times10^2, 9\times10^2, 6\times10^2$
↓	↓	↓
$6\times10^1, 3\times10^3, 9\times10^7$	$9\times10^{-7}, 3\times10^{-3}, 6\times10^{-1}$	$3\times10^2, 6\times10^2, 9\times10^2$

Put in order from least to greatest:

15. $3.2\times10^3, 4.1\times10^2, 5.8\times10^4$

   a. $5.8\times10^4, 4.1\times10^2, 3.2\times10^3$
   b. $3.2\times10^3, 4.1\times10^2, 5.8\times10^4$
   c. $4.1\times10^2, 3.2\times10^3, 5.8\times10^4$
   d. $5.8\times10^4, 3.2\times10^3, 4.1\times10^2$

16. $9.8\times10^{-2}, 7.3\times10^{-5}, 6.4\times10^{-1}$

   a. $6.4\times10^{-1}, 9.8\times10^{-2}, 7.3\times10^{-5}$
   b. $9.8\times10^{-2}, 7.3\times10^{-5}, 6.4\times10^{-1}$
   c. $6.4\times10^{-1}, 7.3\times10^{-5}, 9.8\times10^{-2}$
   d. $7.3\times10^{-5}, 9.8\times10^{-2}, 6.4\times10^{-1}$

17. $3\times10^3, 1\times10^3, 6\times10^3$

   a. $3\times10^3, 1\times10^3, 6\times10^3$
   b. $1\times10^3, 6\times10^3, 3\times10^3$
   c. $1\times10^3, 3\times10^3, 6\times10^3$
   d. $6\times10^3, 3\times10^3, 1\times10^3$

18. $7.8\times10^{-2}, 8.9\times10^{-2}, 3.6\times10^{-2}$

   a. $3.6\times10^{-2}, 7.8\times10^{-2}, 8.9\times10^{-2}$
   b. $7.8\times10^{-2}, 8.9\times10^{-2}, 3.6\times10^{-2}$
   c. $8.9\times10^{-2}, 3.6\times10^{-2}, 7.8\times10^{-2}$
   d. $8.9\times10^{-2}, 7.8\times10^{-2}, 3.6\times10^{-2}$

19. $3.6\times10^{-3}, 3.6\times10^{-4}, 3.6\times10^{-5}$

   a. $3.6\times10^{-4}, 3.6\times10^{-5}, 3.6\times10^{-5}$
   b. $3.6\times10^{-5}, 3.6\times10^{-3}, 3.6\times10^{-5}$
   c. $3.6\times10^{-3}, 3.6\times10^{-4}, 3.6\times10^{-5}$
   d. $3.6\times10^{-5}, 3.6\times10^{-4}, 3.6\times10^{-3}$

20. $1.32\times10^{-1}, 3.21\times10^{-4}, 2.13\times10^{-2}$

   a. $1.32\times10^{-1}, 2.13\times10^{-2}, 3.21\times10^{-4}$
   b. $2.13\times10^{-2}, 3.21\times10^{-4}, 1.32\times10^{-1}$
   c. $3.21\times10^{-4}, 2.13\times10^{-2}, 1.32\times10^{-1}$
   d. $1.32\times10^{-1}, 3.21\times10^{-4}, 2.13\times10^{-2}$

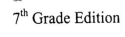

Content Cluster – NUMBER SENSE (Computation Skills)

Objective: Students will add, subtract, multiply and divide rational numbers, integers, fractions and decimals.

> **Parent Tip:** The definition of a rational number is any number that can be represented in the $\frac{a}{b}$ form of two integers a and b, b can **not** be zero.

Addition and Subtraction:

> **Parent Tip:** Remember when **adding** or **subtracting** rational numbers, the denominators must be the same and the rules for adding (subtracting) integers also apply.
>
> $$\frac{^-2}{5} + \frac{3}{4} \;\rightarrow\; \frac{^-8}{20} + \frac{15}{20} = \frac{7}{20}$$

1. $\dfrac{4}{5} + \dfrac{^-3}{5} =$

   a. $\dfrac{1}{10}$

   b. $\dfrac{1}{5}$

   c. $\dfrac{^-1}{5}$

   d. $\dfrac{^-1}{10}$

2. $\dfrac{^-5}{37} - \dfrac{25}{37} =$

   a. $\dfrac{30}{37}$

   b. $\dfrac{20}{37}$

   c. $\dfrac{^-20}{37}$

   d. $\dfrac{^-30}{37}$

3. $\dfrac{^-3}{12} + \dfrac{^-8}{12} =$

   a. $\dfrac{11}{12}$

   b. $\dfrac{5}{12}$

   c. $\dfrac{^-4}{12}$

   d. $\dfrac{^-11}{12}$

4. $\dfrac{4}{15} - \dfrac{^-2}{15} =$

   a. $\dfrac{^-2}{3}$

   b. $\dfrac{2}{3}$

   c. $\dfrac{2}{5}$

   d. $\dfrac{^-2}{5}$

5. $\dfrac{1}{2} + \dfrac{^-1}{3} =$

   a. $\dfrac{1}{6}$

   b. $\dfrac{^-1}{6}$

   c. $\dfrac{1}{5}$

   d. $\dfrac{^-1}{5}$

6. $\dfrac{^-3}{4} - \dfrac{1}{2} =$

   a. $^-1\dfrac{1}{4}$

   b. $\dfrac{^-2}{3}$

   c. $\dfrac{1}{4}$

   d. $\dfrac{^-1}{4}$

7. $\dfrac{3}{8} + \dfrac{^-1}{5} =$

   a. $\dfrac{^-7}{40}$

   b. $\dfrac{^-4}{13}$

   c. $\dfrac{7}{40}$

   d. $\dfrac{2}{13}$

8. $\dfrac{^-3}{8} - \dfrac{1}{3} =$

   a. $\dfrac{4}{5}$

   b. $\dfrac{^-2}{5}$

   c. $\dfrac{^-17}{24}$

   d. $\dfrac{1}{24}$

9. $\dfrac{5}{8} - \dfrac{^-1}{4} =$

   a. $\dfrac{1}{2}$

   b. $\dfrac{7}{8}$

   c. $\dfrac{3}{4}$

   d. $\dfrac{2}{3}$

Multiplication:

> **Parent Tip:** When **multiplying** rational numbers, multiply numerator by numerator and denominator by denominator.
>
> **Remember:**   Positive x Positive = Positive
> Negative x Negative = Positive
> Positive x Negative = Negative
> Negative x Positive = Negative
>
> $$\dfrac{^-1}{5} \times \dfrac{2}{3} = \dfrac{^-1 \times 2}{5 \times 3} = \dfrac{^-2}{15}$$

10. $\dfrac{^-3}{7} \times \dfrac{^-3}{4} =$

   a. $\dfrac{6}{11}$

   b. $\dfrac{^-6}{11}$

   c. $\dfrac{^-9}{28}$

   d. $\dfrac{9}{28}$

11. $\dfrac{^-1}{4} \times \dfrac{3}{11} =$

   a. $\dfrac{1}{11}$

   b. $\dfrac{3}{44}$

   c. $\dfrac{^-3}{44}$

   d. $\dfrac{^-4}{15}$

12. $\dfrac{^-1}{5} \times \dfrac{^-3}{7} =$

   a. $\dfrac{^-3}{35}$

   b. $\dfrac{3}{35}$

   c. $\dfrac{2}{35}$

   d. $\dfrac{^-1}{3}$

13. $\dfrac{4}{9} \times \dfrac{^-1}{5} =$

    a. $\dfrac{^-4}{45}$

    b. $\dfrac{4}{45}$

    c. $\dfrac{^-5}{14}$

    d. $\dfrac{3}{4}$

14. $\dfrac{^-8}{7} \times \dfrac{^-5}{3} =$

    a. $^-1\dfrac{19}{21}$

    b. $1\dfrac{19}{21}$

    c. $^-1\dfrac{3}{10}$

    d. $\dfrac{^-3}{4}$

15. $\dfrac{^-6}{7} \times \dfrac{^-2}{3} =$

    a. $\dfrac{4}{7}$

    b. $\dfrac{^-4}{7}$

    c. $\dfrac{4}{5}$

    d. $\dfrac{^-4}{5}$

Division:

> **Parent Tip:** When **dividing** rational numbers, multiply the first fraction by the reciprocal (turn the fraction upside down) of the second fraction.
>
> $\dfrac{2}{5} \div \dfrac{^-3}{4}$, since $\dfrac{^-4}{3}$ is the reciprocal of $\dfrac{^-3}{4}$ then; $\dfrac{2}{5} \times \dfrac{^-4}{3} = \dfrac{^-8}{15}$

16. $\dfrac{^-3}{2} \div \dfrac{^-1}{4} =$

    a. $^-6$

    b. 6

    c. $\dfrac{^-3}{8}$

    d. $\dfrac{3}{8}$

17. $\dfrac{3}{8} \div \dfrac{^-6}{5} =$

    a. $\dfrac{^-9}{13}$

    b. $\dfrac{^-5}{16}$

    c. $\dfrac{5}{16}$

    d. $\dfrac{9}{13}$

18. $\dfrac{^-7}{12} \div \dfrac{5}{4} =$

    a. $\dfrac{^-7}{15}$

    b. $\dfrac{7}{15}$

    c. $\dfrac{^-3}{4}$

    d. $\dfrac{3}{8}$

19. $\dfrac{7}{10} \div \dfrac{^-7}{6} =$

    a. $\dfrac{3}{5}$ c. $\dfrac{^-7}{8}$

    b. $\dfrac{^-3}{5}$ d. $\dfrac{7}{8}$

20. $\dfrac{^-14}{15} \div \dfrac{^-7}{9} =$

    a. $^-1\dfrac{1}{6}$ c. $1\dfrac{1}{5}$

    b. $1\dfrac{1}{6}$ d. $^-1\dfrac{1}{5}$

> **Parent Tip:** Remember, always **reduce** the answers to the lowest term!

7th Grade Edition

CONTENT CLUSTER – Number Sense (Rational Numbers, Integers, Fractions and Decimals)

Decimals -

> **Parent Tip:** When working with **adding** or **subtracting** decimals, you must make sure that the decimals are lined up and add zeros when necessary.
>
> $34.04 + 5.2 + 12.901$
>
> 34.040 ← add a zero
> 5.200 ← add 2 zeros
> $+12.901$
>
> $154.3 - 63.067$
>
> 154.300 ← add 2 zeros
> -63.067

Addition and Subtraction:

21. $9.168 + 3.51 =$
    a. 9.519
    b. 9.678
    c. 12.519
    d. 12.678

22. $17.6 + 13.372 =$
    a. 30.972
    b. 30.548
    c. 29.972
    d. 29.548

23. $8.3 + 2.06 + 7.319 =$
    a. 17.679
    b. 7.679
    c. 7.608
    d. 17.608

24. $48.6 - 17.3 =$
    a. 65.9
    b. 65.3
    c. 31.3
    d. 30.3

25. $52.8 - 6.04 =$
    a. 46.76
    b. 46.84
    c. 56.76
    d. 56.84

26. $4.03 - 3.806 =$
    a. 1.224
    b. 1.236
    c. 0.236
    d. 0.224

> **Parent Tip:** When working with **multiplying** decimals, there must be the same amount of digits after the decimal point in the answer as there are digits after the decimal points in the two numbers being multiplied.
>
> 12.1 ← **one** digit after the decimal point
> $\times 1.02$ ← **two** digits after the decimal point
> 12.342 ← **three** digits after the decimal point

Multiplication:

27. $0.5 \times 0.7 =$
    a. 3.5
    b. 1.2
    c. 0.12
    d. 0.35

28. $3.02 \times 0.2 =$
    a. 0.304
    b. 0.604
    c. 3.22
    d. 6.04

29. $0.5 \times 0.15 =$
    a. 7.5
    b. 0.75
    c. 0.075
    d. 0.0075

30. $52.9 \times 12 =$
    a. 157.7
    b. 158.7
    c. 634.8
    d. 624.8

31. $6.5 \times 0.9 =$
    a. 4.85
    b. 4.95
    c. 5.75
    d. 5.85

32. $21.7 \times 4.5 =$
    a. 97.55
    b. 97.65
    c. 107.55
    d. 107.65

Parent Tip: When dividing with decimals, you must clear the decimal point in the divisor (the number dividing the other number). To do this, move the decimal point to the right until it is at the end of the number. Once you have done that, count the number of places you moved it and move the decimal in the dividend (the number being divided) the same amount of times. Now divide moving the decimal point straight up into the quotient (answer).

$0.7\overline{)2.87}$ → the divisor, 0.7, has a decimal point and must be moved over to the right once.

↓

$7\overline{)28.7}$ → since 0.7 became 7, 2.87 becomes 28.7 by moving the decimal point also.

The quotient (answer):

$$\begin{array}{r} 4.1 \\ \hline 7{\overline{)28.7}} \end{array}$$

Division:

33. $2.68 \div 4 =$

   a. 0.67
   b. 0.067
   c. 6.7
   d. 6.2

34. $9.42 \div 6 =$

   a. 1.57
   b. 15.7
   c. 0.157
   d. 0.0157

35. $39.6 \div 0.9 =$

   a. 0.044
   b. 0.44
   c. 4.4
   d. 44

36. $2.1 \div 0.25 =$

   a. 0.084
   b. 0.84
   c. 8.4
   d. 84

37. $0.46 \div 0.05 =$

   a. 0.92
   b. 9.2
   c. 92
   d. 920

38. $48 \div 0.06 =$

   a. 8
   b. 80
   c. 800
   d. 8000

CONTENT CLUSTER – Number Sense (Rational Numbers, Integers, Fractions and Decimals)

Fractions –

> **Parent Tip:** Remember when adding or subtracting fractions, the denominators **MUST** be the same. Once you find the common denominator and change the fractions, **only add or subtract the numerators**, leaving the denominator the same. **Note:** Always Reduce Your Answer!

Addition and Subtraction:

39. $\dfrac{4}{5} + \dfrac{7}{5} =$

   a. $1\dfrac{2}{5}$

   b. $1\dfrac{1}{10}$

   c. $2\dfrac{1}{10}$

   d. $2\dfrac{1}{5}$

40. $\dfrac{39}{37} - \dfrac{15}{37} =$

   a. $\dfrac{24}{74}$

   b. $\dfrac{24}{37}$

   c. $1\dfrac{17}{37}$

   d. $\dfrac{17}{37}$

41. $\dfrac{1}{12} + \dfrac{7}{12} =$

   a. $\dfrac{3}{4}$

   b. $\dfrac{2}{3}$

   c. $\dfrac{1}{2}$

   d. $\dfrac{8}{24}$

42. $\dfrac{3}{4} - \dfrac{2}{5} =$

   a. $\dfrac{7}{20}$

   b. $\dfrac{1}{2}$

   c. $\dfrac{2}{5}$

   d. $\dfrac{11}{20}$

43. $\dfrac{3}{8} + \dfrac{4}{7} =$

   a. $\dfrac{7}{15}$

   b. $\dfrac{7}{56}$

   c. $\dfrac{53}{56}$

   d. $\dfrac{7}{8}$

44. $\dfrac{5}{8} - \dfrac{3}{10} =$

   a. $\dfrac{4}{9}$

   b. $\dfrac{37}{40}$

   c. $\dfrac{13}{40}$

   d. $\dfrac{1}{4}$

CONTENT CLUSTER – Number Sense (Rational Numbers, Integers, Fractions and Decimals)

> **Parent Tip:** When multiplying fractions, simply multiply numerators by numerators and denominators by denominators. **Note:** Always Reduce Your Answer!

Multiplication:

45. $\frac{4}{9} \times \frac{2}{5} =$

  a. $\frac{1}{7}$

  b. $\frac{3}{7}$

  c. $\frac{6}{45}$

  d. $\frac{8}{45}$

46. $\frac{3}{4} \times \frac{8}{11} =$

  a. $\frac{6}{11}$

  b. $\frac{11}{15}$

  c. $\frac{1}{4}$

  d. $\frac{8}{11}$

47. $\frac{5}{6} \times \frac{11}{13} =$

  a. $\frac{16}{78}$

  b. $\frac{55}{78}$

  c. $\frac{16}{19}$

  d. $\frac{55}{87}$

48. $\frac{4}{9} \times \frac{7}{8} =$

  a. $\frac{7}{18}$

  b. $\frac{11}{17}$

  c. $\frac{2}{3}$

  d. $\frac{3}{17}$

49. $\frac{10}{7} \times \frac{14}{2} =$

  a. $3\frac{2}{9}$

  b. 10

  c. $1\frac{5}{7}$

  d. $2\frac{2}{3}$

50. $\frac{6}{9} \times \frac{18}{27} =$

  a. $\frac{2}{3}$

  b. $\frac{4}{9}$

  c. 3

  d. $\frac{2}{9}$

Parent Tip: When dividing with fractions, multiply the dividend (the first fraction) by the reciprocal of the divisor (the second fraction). Reciprocal is when you turn the fraction upside down.

Note: Always Reduce Your Answer!

$$\frac{7}{8} \div \frac{3}{4} = \quad \rightarrow \quad \frac{7}{8} \times \frac{4}{3} = \quad \frac{28}{24} \quad = \quad \frac{7}{6} \quad = \quad 1\frac{1}{6}$$

the reciprocal of $\frac{3}{4}$ is $\frac{4}{3}$

Division:

51. $\frac{3}{4} \div \frac{1}{6} =$

   a. $2\frac{1}{4}$

   b. $\frac{1}{2}$

   c. $4\frac{1}{2}$

   d. $2\frac{1}{2}$

52. $\frac{3}{7} \div \frac{3}{5} =$

   a. $\frac{6}{12}$

   b. $\frac{9}{35}$

   c. $\frac{5}{7}$

   d. $\frac{7}{8}$

53. $\frac{5}{12} \div \frac{5}{4} =$

   a. $\frac{5}{8}$

   b. $\frac{25}{48}$

   c. $\frac{3}{4}$

   d. $\frac{1}{3}$

54. $\frac{7}{8} \div \frac{7}{6} =$

   a. $1\frac{1}{48}$

   b. $\frac{3}{4}$

   c. $\frac{4}{5}$

   d. $\frac{7}{24}$

55. $\frac{14}{15} \div \frac{8}{9} =$

   a. $1\frac{1}{20}$

   b. $\frac{11}{12}$

   c. $\frac{112}{135}$

   d. $1\frac{1}{5}$

56. $\frac{9}{16} \div \frac{8}{9} =$

   a. $\frac{17}{25}$

   b. $1\frac{1}{2}$

   c. $\frac{81}{128}$

   d. $\frac{3}{4}$

CONTENT CLUSTER – Number Sense (Rational Numbers, Integers, Fractions and Decimals)

Positive and Negative Numbers (Integers) –

Parent Tip: Adding numbers with the same signs (both + or both -), keep the sign the same and just add the numbers → $^-4 + ^-5 = ^-9$. When the signs are different, keep the sign of the larger number (without looking at the sign) and subtract the two numbers for the value → $^-15 + 8 = ^-7$. Since 15 is greater than 8, your answer is negative and the difference between 15 and 8 which is 7.

Addition:

57. $^-4 + ^-8 =$

    a. $^-4$
    b. $^-12$
    c. 12
    d. 4

58. $^-26 + ^-9 =$

    a. $^-17$
    b. $^-35$
    c. 17
    d. 35

59. $^-30 + ^-40 =$

    a. 10
    b. 70
    c. $^-10$
    d. $^-70$

60. $^-15 + 17 =$

    a. $^-2$
    b. 2
    c. $^-32$
    d. 32

61. $^-43 + 66 =$

    a. $^-109$
    b. $^-23$
    c. 23
    d. 109

62. $33 + ^-70 =$

    a. 103
    b. $^-103$
    c. $^-37$
    d. 37

Parent Tip: The first thing to do with a subtraction problem is change it into an addition problem. Leave the minuend (the first number) alone, change the subtrahend (the second number) to its opposite and then add the two number applying the addition of integers rules.

$^-13 - ^-5 =$ → leave $^-13$ alone, change $^-5$ to 5,

now add the two numbers together → $^-13 + 5 = ^-8$

Subtraction:

63. $^-23 - ^-4 =$

    a. $^-27$
    b. $^-19$
    c. 19
    d. 27

64. $^-78 - 19 =$

    a. $^-97$
    b. 97
    c. 59
    d. $^-59$

65. $^-35 - 35 =$

    a. $^-70$
    b. 70
    c. 0
    d. 75

66. $43 - {}^-17 =$

   a. 60
   b. ${}^-60$
   c. ${}^-26$
   d. 26

67. ${}^-75 - 22 =$

   a. 63
   b. ${}^-63$
   c. ${}^-97$
   d. 97

68. $56 - {}^-34 =$

   a. ${}^-90$
   b. 90
   c. ${}^-22$
   d. 22

Parent Tip: When multiplying or dividing integers, the sign rules for the answers are the same. If you multiply or divide numbers with the same sign, the answer will be positive.

$${}^-5 \times {}^-7 = 35 \quad \text{and} \quad {}^-56 \div {}^-14 = 4$$

And if you multiply or divide numbers with different signs, the answer will be negative.

$${}^-12 \times 4 = {}^-48 \quad \text{and} \quad 63 \div {}^-9 = {}^-7$$

Multiplication:

69. ${}^-4 \times 6 =$

   a. 18
   b. ${}^-18$
   c. ${}^-24$
   d. 24

70. ${}^-13 \times {}^-4 =$

   a. ${}^-42$
   b. 42
   c. ${}^-52$
   d. 52

71. $20 \times {}^-15 =$

   a. ${}^-300$
   b. 300
   c. ${}^-400$
   d. 350

72. $14 \times 25 =$

   a. ${}^-350$
   b. 350
   c. ${}^-325$
   d. 325

73. ${}^-151 \times {}^-9 =$

   a. ${}^-957$
   b. 957
   c. ${}^-1357$
   d. 1357

74. ${}^-84 \times 17 =$

   a. 1428
   b. 1328
   c. ${}^-1328$
   d. ${}^-1428$

Division:

75. ${}^-125 \div {}^-25 =$

   a. ${}^-5$
   b. 5
   c. ${}^-4$
   d. 4

76. ${}^-372 \div {}^-6 =$

   a. ${}^-62$
   b. 62
   c. ${}^-72$
   d. 72

77. ${}^-690 \div {}^-23 =$

   a. ${}^-33$
   b. 33
   c. 30
   d. ${}^-30$

CONTENT CLUSTER – Number Sense (Rational Numbers, Integers, Fractions and Decimals)

78. $^-84 \div 6 =$

    a. 14
    b. $^-14$
    c. 16
    d. $^-16$

79. $^-93 \div \,^-3 =$

    a. $^-31$
    b. 31
    c. $^-32$
    d. 32

80. $196 \div \,^-14 =$

    a. 13
    b. $^-13$
    c. 14
    d. $^-14$

Content Cluster – NUMBER SENSE (Whole Number Powers)

Objective: Students will take rational numbers to whole number powers.

Parent Tip: First change the rational number into a decimal, then put into scientific notation and finally, change the negative exponent to a positive by inverting it.

rational number	decimal form	scientific notation	whole number power

Example: $\dfrac{^{-}1}{2}$ $\rightarrow$ $^{-}0.5$ $\rightarrow$ $^{-}5 \times 10^{-1}$ $\rightarrow$ $^{-}5 \times \dfrac{1}{10^{1}}$

(note: when you invert 10^{-4} to make it $\dfrac{1}{10^{4}}$, the **exponent becomes positive**)

Convert to whole number powers:

1. $\dfrac{2}{5}$

    a. 4×10^{1}

    b. 4×10^{0}

    c. $4 \times \dfrac{1}{10^{1}}$

    d. $4 \times \dfrac{1}{10^{2}}$

2. $\dfrac{^{-}5}{8}$

    a. $^{-}6.25 \times 10^{1}$

    b. $^{-}6.25 \times \dfrac{1}{10^{1}}$

    c. $^{-}6.25 \times \dfrac{1}{10^{2}}$

    d. $^{-}6.25 \times \dfrac{1}{10^{3}}$

3. $\dfrac{^{-}1}{125}$

    a. $^{-}8 \times \dfrac{1}{10^{1}}$

    b. $^{-}8 \times \dfrac{1}{10^{2}}$

    c. $^{-}8 \times \dfrac{1}{10^{3}}$

    d. $^{-}8 \times \dfrac{1}{10^{4}}$

4. $\dfrac{7}{250}$

    a. $2.8 \times \dfrac{1}{10^{2}}$

    b. $2.8 \times \dfrac{1}{10^{1}}$

    c. 2.8×10^{1}

    d. 2.8×10^{2}

5. $\dfrac{^{-}1}{16}$

    a. $^{-}6.25 \times 10^{2}$

    b. $^{-}6.25 \times 10^{1}$

    c. $^{-}6.25 \times \dfrac{1}{10^{1}}$

    d. $^{-}6.25 \times \dfrac{1}{10^{2}}$

6. $\dfrac{15}{16}$

    a. 9.375×10^{2}

    b. 9.375×10^{1}

    c. $9.375 \times \dfrac{1}{10^{1}}$

    d. $9.375 \times \dfrac{1}{10^{2}}$

Content Cluster – NUMBER SENSE (Convert Fractions)

Objective: Students will convert fractions to decimals and percents.

Parent Tip: When converting a fraction into a decimal, divide the numerator (top number) by the denominator (bottom number).

Example: $\dfrac{1}{2}$ → $2\overline{)1.0}$ gives 0.5, -10 → 0.5 is the decimal form for $\dfrac{1}{2}$.

$\dfrac{2}{3}$ → $3\overline{)2.00}$ gives 0.66, -18, 20, -18 → $0.\overline{6}$ is the decimal form for $\dfrac{2}{3}$.

Change the following fractions into decimals:

1. $\dfrac{3}{4}$

   a. 0.34
   b. 0.75
   c. 1.33
   d. 1.25

2. $\dfrac{5}{8}$

   a. 0.625
   b. 0.580
   c. 0.850
   d. 1.600

3. $\dfrac{3}{5}$

   a. 0.3
   b. 0.5
   c. 0.6
   d. 1.6

4. $\dfrac{3}{11}$

   a. $0.\overline{27}$
   b. $0.\overline{11}$
   c. $0.\overline{33}$
   d. $3.\overline{66}$

5. $\dfrac{5}{9}$

   a. 0.6
   b. 0.9
   c. 0.5
   d. $0.\overline{5}$

6. $\dfrac{2}{3}$

   a. 0.2
   b. 0.6
   c. 0.3
   d. $0.\overline{6}$

7. $\dfrac{19}{20}$

   a. 0.19
   b. 0.95
   c. 1.05
   d. 0.20

8. $\dfrac{13}{15}$

   a. $0.8\overline{6}$
   b. 0.87
   c. 0.13
   d. 0.15

9. $\dfrac{27}{30}$

   a. $0.\overline{3}$
   b. $0.\overline{6}$
   c. 0.9
   d. $1.\overline{1}$

Parent Tip: When converting a fraction into a percent, change it into a decimal first then move the decimal point **two** times to the right.

Example: $\dfrac{3}{4}$ $\rightarrow$

$$\begin{array}{r} 0.75 \\ 4\overline{)3.00} \\ -\underline{28} \\ 20 \\ -\underline{20} \end{array}$$

$\rightarrow$ 0.<u>75</u> (by moving the decimal) $\rightarrow$ 75%

---

10. $\dfrac{7}{10}$

   a. 40%
   b. 50%
   c. 60%
   d. 70%

11. $\dfrac{3}{5}$

   a. 10%
   b. 30%
   c. 50%
   d. 60%

12. $\dfrac{7}{8}$

   a. 87%
   b. 87.5%
   c. 78%
   d. 75%

13. $\dfrac{11}{12}$

   a. $91.\overline{6}\%$
   b. 92%
   c. 95%
   d. $96.\overline{6}\%$

14. $\dfrac{31}{40}$

   a. 31%
   b. 40%
   c. 77.5%
   d. 78%

15. $\dfrac{60}{90}$

   a. $56.\overline{6}\%$
   b. 60%
   c. $66.\overline{6}\%$
   d. 70%

Content Cluster – NUMBER SENSE (Use Decimals/Percents)

Objective: Students will use decimals and percents in estimation, computation and application.

> **Parent Tip:** When estimating, see how close the decimal or percent is to a known fraction. For example, 23% is close to ¼ (25%) so 23% of 40 is approximately 10 and 77% is close to ¾ (75%) so 77% of 60 is approximately 45.

Estimate the following:

1. 12% of 50.

   a. 5
   b. 10
   c. 12
   d. 15

2. 33% of 75.

   a. 25
   b. 30
   c. 35
   d. 40

3. 0.19 of 120.

   a. 12
   b. 15
   c. 20
   d. 24

4. 0.82 of 80.

   a. 40
   b. 50
   c. 64
   d. 72

5. 67% of 90.

   a. 55
   b. 60
   c. 65
   d. 70

6. 145% of 36.

   a. 32
   b. 40
   c. 48
   d. 54

7. 0.53 of 80.

   a. 40
   b. 50
   c. 60
   d. 70

8. 48% of 300.

   a. 50
   b. 100
   c. 150
   d. 200

9. 0.97 of 45.

   a. 30
   b. 35
   c. 40
   d. 45

Parent Tip: When working with percents, there are <u>two ways</u> to solve for the unknown. You can turn the word problem into an equation or set up a proportion.

A) The Equation Method –

What is 10% of 50.
↓ ↓ ↓ ↓ ↓
$x = 0.10 \times 50$ therefore $x = 5$

B) The Proportion Method –

What is 10% of 50.

$$\frac{\%}{100} = \frac{"is"}{"of"} \rightarrow \frac{10}{100} = \frac{x}{50} \rightarrow 100x = 500 \rightarrow x = 5$$

Solve the following:

10. What is 30% of 60?

   a.   9
   b.   18
   c.   24
   d.   30

11. 20% of 80 is what?

   a.   8
   b.   10
   c.   12
   d.   16

12. 12 is what percent of 24?

   a.   25%
   b.   30%
   c.   50%
   d.   60%

13. 60 is what percent of 90?

   a.   50%
   b.   60%
   c. $66.\overline{3}\%$
   d. $66.\overline{6}\%$

14. What percent of 75 is 20?

   a. $23.\overline{3}\%$
   b.   25%
   c. $26.\overline{6}\%$
   d. $30.\overline{3}\%$

15. What percent of 10 is 20?

   a.   200%
   b.   150%
   c.   100%
   d.   50%

Content Cluster – NUMBER SENSE (Rational or Irrational)

Objective: Students will differentiate between rational and irrational numbers.

Parent Tip:
Rational numbers are numbers that when put into decimal form and will either <u>terminate</u> (come out evenly when divided) or <u>repeat</u> (a number or set of numbers will repeat in a specific pattern).
Irrational numbers are numbers that when put into decimal form go on forever without having any specific pattern

---

Determine if the number is rational or irrational:

1. $\dfrac{1}{2}$

    a. rational
    b. irrational

2. $\dfrac{1}{3}$

    a. rational
    b. irrational

3. $\dfrac{22}{7}$

    a. rational
    b. irrational

4. $\dfrac{3}{4}$

    a. rational
    b. irrational

5. $\dfrac{1}{7}$

    a. rational
    b. irrational

6. $\sqrt{2}$

    a. rational
    b. irrational

7. 7.5

    a. rational
    b. irrational

8. $\dfrac{5}{9}$

    a. rational
    b. irrational

9. $\sqrt{65}$

    a. rational
    b. irrational

Content Cluster – NUMBER SENSE (Terminating/Repeating)

Objective: Students will know that fractions are either a terminating or repeating decimals and be able to convert fractions to decimals or decimals to fractions.

Parent Tip:
Definitions:
A **terminating decimal** is a decimal that ends when you convert a fraction into a decimal.
A **repeating decimal** is a decimal that goes on forever (in no particular pattern) when you convert a fraction into a decimal.

Determine which is terminating or repeating:

1. $\dfrac{2}{3}$

    a. terminating
    b. repeating

2. $\dfrac{2}{4}$

    a. terminating
    b. repeating

3. $\dfrac{4}{9}$

    a. terminating
    b. repeating

4. $\dfrac{3}{7}$

    a. terminating
    b. repeating

5. $\dfrac{7}{8}$

    a. terminating
    b. repeating

6. $\dfrac{4}{5}$

    a. terminating
    b. repeating

7. $\dfrac{11}{18}$

    a. terminating
    b. repeating

8. $\dfrac{4}{27}$

    a. terminating
    b. repeating

9. $\dfrac{13}{65}$

    a. terminating
    b. repeating

Content Cluster – NUMBER SENSE (Converting – Decimal/Fractions)

Objective: Students will be able to convert fractions to decimals or decimals to fractions.

Parent Tip: To convert a fraction to a decimal, just divide the numerator (top number) by the denominator (bottom number).

$$\text{Example: } \frac{3}{4} \rightarrow 4\overline{)3.00} \rightarrow 0.75$$

Change into decimal form:

1. $\dfrac{2}{5}$

    a. 0.2
    b. 0.4
    c. 0.5
    d. 2.5

2. $\dfrac{7}{8}$

    a. 1.143
    b. 0.780
    c. 0.870
    d. 0.875

3. $\dfrac{3}{6}$

    a. 0.3
    b. 0.5
    c. 0.6
    d. 2.0

4. $\dfrac{12}{25}$

    a. 0.12
    b. 0.25
    c. 0.48
    d. 2.08

5. $\dfrac{13}{65}$

    a. 0.20
    b. 0.13
    c. 0.65
    d. 5.00

6. $\dfrac{8}{200}$

    a. 0.02
    b. 0.04
    c. 0.08
    d. 0.28

Parent Tip: When you read the decimal number, <u>read it correctly</u> and you will know the value of the denominator.

Example: 0.125; read it - one hundred twenty-five <u>thousandths</u>,

so the denominator is 1000 $\rightarrow \dfrac{125}{1000}$

---

7. 0.33

    a. $\dfrac{33}{10}$
    b. $\dfrac{33}{100}$
    c. $\dfrac{33}{1000}$
    d. $\dfrac{33}{10000}$

8. 0.7

    a. $\dfrac{7}{10}$
    b. $\dfrac{7}{100}$
    c. $\dfrac{7}{1000}$
    d. $\dfrac{7}{10000}$

9. 0.325

    a. $\dfrac{325}{10}$
    b. $\dfrac{325}{100}$
    c. $\dfrac{325}{1000}$
    d. $\dfrac{325}{10000}$

10. 0.08

    a. $\frac{8}{10}$

    b. $\frac{8}{100}$

    c. $\frac{8}{1000}$

    d. $\frac{8}{10000}$

11. 0.0036

    a. $\frac{36}{10}$

    b. $\frac{36}{100}$

    c. $\frac{36}{1000}$

    d. $\frac{36}{10000}$

12. 0.0104

    a. $\frac{104}{10}$

    b. $\frac{104}{100}$

    c. $\frac{104}{1000}$

    d. $\frac{104}{10000}$

Content Cluster – NUMBER SENSE (Percent Increase/Decrease)

Objective: Students will be able to calculate percent of increase and decrease of a quantity.

Parent Tip: The percent of <u>increase</u> or <u>decrease</u> is the same as figuring the percent of change.

Example: $\dfrac{\text{The amount of change}}{\text{Original Amount}} \times 100$ = Percent of Increase/Decrease

(**note:** the amount of change is the difference between the original amount and the new amount)

Find the Percent of Increase/Decrease:

1. from 40 to 50
   a. 20% increase
   b. 25% increase
   c. 20% decrease
   d. 25% decrease

2. from 70 to 30
   a. 43% increase
   b. 57% increase
   c. 43% decrease
   d. 57% decrease

3. from 50% to 75%
   a. 25% increase
   b. 50% increase
   c. 25% decrease
   d. 50% decrease

4. from 24 to 28
   a. 17% increase
   b. 17% decrease
   c. 24% increase
   d. 28% decrease

5. from 25 to 24
   a. 4% increase
   b. 4% decrease
   c. 25% increase
   d. 25% decrease

6. from 51 to 68
   a. 33% increase
   b. 33% decrease
   c. 67% increase
   d. 67% decrease

7. from $1.25 to $1.50
   a. 25% increase
   b. 25% decrease
   c. 20% increase
   d. 20% decrease

8. from 12 to 21
   a. 67% increase
   b. 67% decrease
   c. 75% increase
   d. 75% decrease

9. from $100 to $60
   a. 40% increase
   b. 40% decrease
   c. 60% increase
   d. 60% decrease

Content Cluster – NUMBER SENSE (Discounts/Markups)

Objective: Students will solve problems that involve discounts, markups, commission, profit and simple compound interest.

Parent Tip: These are the type of problems where you will apply the rules of working with percents. Once you solve for the percent of discount or markup, you either subtract form the original amount (discount) or add to the original amount (markup) to get the final solution for the problem.

Example: 10% discount on a $20.00 item.

Solution: $20 x 10% → $20.00 x 0.1 = $2.00 now subtract
$2.00 from $20.00 → $18.00 is the new cost.
(if it is a markup, add to the original item)

Find the new cost after the discount or markup:

1. $40.00 item, 25% discount

    a. $20.00
    b. $25.00
    c. $30.00
    d. $35.00

2. $60.00 item, 10% markup

    a. $63.00
    b. $66.00
    c. $70.00
    d. $72.00

3. $32.00 item, 15% discount

    a. $36.80
    b. $27.20
    c. $27.80
    d. $25.20

4. $875.00 item, 30% markup

    a. $837.50
    b. $937.50
    c. $1037.50
    d. $1137.50

Parent Tip: A commission is the amount of money made on the sale of an item, it is based on a percent of the items selling price. When figuring a commission, multiply the amount of the sale by the percent of the commission

Example: $500 item, 2% commission → $500 x 0.02 = $10.00 commission

---

Find the amount of commission:

5. $26,500 car, 6% commission

    a. $1590
    b. $2590
    c. $27,090
    d. $28,090

6. $250,000 house, 3% commission

    a. $5500
    b. $6000
    c. $6500
    d. $7500

7. $56,750 boat, 4% commission

    a. $2170
    b. $2270
    c. $2375
    d. $2500

8. $3,500,000 house, 2% commission

    a. $7,000
    b. $70,000
    c. $700,000
    d. $777,000

Parent Tip: With compound interest, the amount of the principal (money in the account) will increase each year because the interest for that year is put back into the account and the next year's interest is figured on the new amount.

Example: **Interest** = **Principal** (money) x **Rate** (percent) x **Time** (years)

    (**note:** with compound interest, the **years** represent the number of times the principal is multiplied by the rate)

Find the final amount of money in the account.
$1000 (principal), **4%** (rate) per year, compounded **over 3 years**.

    $1000 x 0.04 = $40.00 → $1000 + $40 = $1040 (new principal)
    $1040 x 0.04 = $41.60 → $1040 + $41.60 = $1081.60 (new principal)
    $1081.60 x 0.04 = $43.26 → $1081.60 + $43.26 = $1124.86 (final principal)

Find the Final Principal:

9. $20,000 (principal), 3% (rate) per year.
Interest compounded over 2 years.

    a. $20,600
    b. $21,200
    c. $21,218
    d. $21,418

10. $100,000 (principal), 5% (rate) per year.
Interest compounded over 4 years.

    a. $126,628.16
    b. $121,550.63
    c. $120,000.00
    d. $115,762.50

Content Cluster – NUMBER SENSE (Squares and Roots)

Objective: Students will use the inverse relationship between raising to a power and root extraction (square root) for a perfect square.

> **Parent Tip:** The definition of squaring a number is to multiply the number by itself.
>
> Example: $5^2 = 5 \times 5 = 25$
>
> The definition of finding the square root of a number is to find two of the **same numbers** (factors) that when multiply together make the number.
>
> Example: $\sqrt{64} = 8$ because $8 \times 8 = 64$ (any square root that equals a whole number is a "**perfect square**")

Find the square root of the following numbers:

1. $\sqrt{25}$

   a. 4
   b. 5
   c. 6
   d. 7

2. $\sqrt{81}$

   a. 6
   b. 7
   c. 8
   d. 9

3. $\sqrt{121}$

   a. 11
   b. 12
   c. 13
   d. 14

4. $\sqrt{49}$

   a. 6
   b. 7
   c. 8
   d. 8

5. $\sqrt{100}$

   a. 8
   b. 9
   c. 10
   d. 11

6. $\sqrt{225}$

   a. 12
   b. 13
   c. 14
   d. 15

7. $\sqrt{400}$

   a. 20
   b. 25
   c. 30
   d. 40

8. $\sqrt{10,000}$

   a. 25
   b. 50
   c. 100
   d. 200

9. $\sqrt{6400}$

   a. 70
   b. 80
   c. 90
   d. 95

Content Cluster – NUMBER SENSE (Negative Exponents)

Objective: Students will understand negative whole number exponents. Multiply and divide expressions involving exponents with a common base.

Parent Tip: The rules for negative exponents (with a common base) are the same as the rules for positive exponents (with a common base).

Rules: 1) When multiplying → keep the base and add the exponents
2) When dividing → keep the base and subtract the exponents

Example: $3^{-4} \times 3^{-5} = 3^{-9}$

$$4^{-6} \div 4^{-2} = 4^{-4} \quad \text{or} \quad \frac{4^{-6}}{4^{-2}} = 4^{-4}$$

Simplify the following:

1. $(10^{-1})(10^{-4})$

   a. 10^{-3}
   b. 10^{-5}
   c. 10^{-6}
   d. 10^{3}

2. $8^{-4} \div 8^{-1}$

   a. 8^{-1}
   b. 8^{-2}
   c. 8^{-3}
   d. 8^{-4}

3. $6^{-2} \times 6^{-2}$

   a. 6^{-1}
   b. 6^{-2}
   c. 6^{-3}
   d. 6^{-4}

4. $\dfrac{13^{-6}}{13^{-5}}$

   a. 13^{-3}
   b. 13^{-2}
   c. 13^{-1}
   d. 13^{1}

5. $20^{-8} \cdot 20^{-1}$

   a. 20^{-9}
   b. 20^{-8}
   c. 20^{-7}
   d. 20^{-6}

6. $2^{-3} \div 2^{-4}$

   a. 2^{2}
   b. 2^{1}
   c. 2^{-1}
   d. 2^{-2}

7. $5^{-2} \times 5^{-3} \times 5^{-5}$

   a. 5^{-7}
   b. 5^{-8}
   c. 5^{-9}
   d. 5^{-10}

8. $\dfrac{3^{-5}}{3^{-2}} \cdot 3^{-4}$

   a. 3^{-4}
   b. 3^{-5}
   c. 3^{-6}
   d. 3^{-7}

9. $\dfrac{4^{-2} \cdot 4^{-3}}{4^{-5}}$

   a. 4^{0}
   b. 4^{-1}
   c. 4^{-2}
   d. 4^{-3}

Content Cluster – NUMBER SENSE (Estimate Square Roots)

Objective: Students will determine, without a calculator, the two integers between which the square root of the not perfect square lies and why.

Parent Tip: When you are finding which to integers a square root lies, you have to know some of the perfect squares.

Perfect Squares

$\sqrt{1} = 1$ $\sqrt{64} = 8$

$\sqrt{4} = 2$ $\sqrt{81} = 9$

$\sqrt{9} = 3$ $\sqrt{100} = 10$

$\sqrt{16} = 4$ $\sqrt{121} = 11$

$\sqrt{25} = 5$ $\sqrt{144} = 12$

$\sqrt{36} = 6$ $\sqrt{169} = 13$

$\sqrt{49} = 7$ $\sqrt{196} = 14$

$\sqrt{225} = 15$

Since the $\sqrt{40}$ is between the $\sqrt{36}$ and $\sqrt{49}$, then the square root is between **6 and 7**.

Between which two integers does the square root lie:

1. $\sqrt{13}$

     a. 3 and 4
     b. 4 and 5
     c. 5 and 6
     d. 6 and 7

2. $\sqrt{45}$

     a. 3 and 4
     b. 4 and 5
     c. 5 and 6
     d. 6 and 7

3. $\sqrt{23}$

     a. 3 and 4
     b. 4 and 5
     c. 5 and 6
     d. 6 and 7

4. $\sqrt{30}$

     a. 3 and 4
     b. 4 and 5
     c. 5 and 6
     d. 6 and 7

5. $\sqrt{91}$

     a. 7 and 8
     b. 8 and 9
     c. 9 and 10
     d. 10 and 11

6. $\sqrt{113}$

     a. 7 and 8
     b. 8 and 9
     c. 9 and 10
     d. 10 and 11

7. $\sqrt{143}$

     a. 11 and 12
     b. 12 and 13
     c. 13 and 14
     d. 14 and 15

8. $\sqrt{160}$

     a. 11 and 12
     b. 12 and 13
     c. 13 and 14
     d. 14 and 15

Content Cluster – NUMBER SENSE (Absolute Value)

Objective: Students will understand the meaning of the absolute value of a number and determine the absolute values of real numbers.

> **Parent Tip:** The definition of the absolute value of a number is the distance that number is from **zero**, <u>regardless of the direction</u>. The symbol for the absolute value is - $\left|^-3\right|$ - this is read "the absolute value of negative three".
>
> Example: $\left|^-3\right| = 3$ because the distance of $^-3$ from 0 is 3.

Find the absolute values of the following:

1. $|3|$

    a. $^-3$
    b. 3

2. $\left|^-13\right|$

    a. 13
    b. $^-13$

3. $|37|$

    a. $^-37$
    b. 37

4. $\left|^-6\right|$

    a. $^-6$
    b. 6

5. $\left|^-17\right|$

    a. 17
    b. $^-17$

6. $|412|$

    a. 412
    b. $^-412$

7. $\left|^-39.4\right|$

    a. $^-39.4$

    b. 39.4

8. $\left|^-0.05\right|$

    a. 0.05

    b. $^-0.05$

9. $\left|\dfrac{1}{2}\right|$

    a. $\dfrac{1}{2}$

    b. $^-\dfrac{1}{2}$

Content Cluster – ALGEBRA AND FUNCTIONS (Verbal to Problem)

Objective: Students will use variables and appropriate operations to write an expression, equation, inequality, or system of equations or inequalities that represent a verbal description.

> Parent Tip: Know what each word is as a symbol, i.e. "is → =", "the sum → +", "the product → x", etc

Word to symbol list:

Addition (+)	Subtraction (–)	Multiplication (x)	Division (÷)
the <u>sum</u> of	the <u>difference</u> of (when)	the <u>product</u> of (when)	the <u>quotient</u> of (when)
the <u>total</u> of	<u>less</u> than	<u>times</u>	<u>divided</u> by
<u>added</u> to	<u>smaller</u> than	<u>multiplied</u> by	
<u>increased</u> by	<u>subtracted</u> from		
<u>greater</u> than	<u>decreased</u> by		
<u>larger</u> than			

Write as algebraic expressions:

> **Parent Tip:** Algebraic expressions **do not** have a mathematical verb, that is one of the symbols =, <, or >

1. The product of fifty-three and n

   a. 53 + n
   b. n - 53
   c. 53n
   d. 53 ÷ n

2. Twelve larger than x

   a. x + 12
   b. 12 - x
   c. 12x
   d. 12 ÷ x

3. The quotient when b is divided by seventy-nine

   a. b + 79
   b. b - 79
   c. 79b
   d. b ÷ 79

4. Eighteen less than w

   a. w + 18
   b. w - 18
   c. 18w
   d. 18 ÷ w

5. The sum of ninety-four and g

   a. 94 + g
   b. 94 - g
   c. 94g
   d. 94 ÷ g

6. t increased by twenty

   a. t + 20
   b. t - 20
   c. 20t
   d. t ÷ 20

7. Fourteen times a

   a. 14 + a
   b. 14 - a
   c. 14a
   d. 14 ÷ a

8. Eight-one divided by d

   a. 81 + d
   b. 81 - d
   c. 81d
   d. 81 ÷ d

9. Total of forty-two and p

   a. 42 + p
   b. 42 - p
   c. 42p
   d. 42 ÷ p

Write as algebraic sentences:

Parent Tip: Algebraic sentences **must have** a mathematical verb, that is one of the symbols =, <, or >

More words to symbols – "is equal to → =", "is greater than → >" and "is less than → <"

---

10. Three greater than y is greater than fifteen.

   a. y + 3 > 15
   b. y - 3 > 15
   c. 3y > 15
   d. y ÷ 3 > 15

11. Two less than m is equal to eleven.

   a. m + 2 = 11
   b. m - 2 = 11
   c. 2m = 11
   d. m ÷ 2 = 11

12. The difference between h and fifteen is less than thirty.

   a. h + 15 < 30
   b. h - 15 < 30
   c. 15h < 30
   d. h ÷ 15 < 30

13. The total of k and thirty is greater than sixty.

   a. k + 30 > 60
   b. k - 30 > 60
   c. 30k > 60
   d. k ÷ 30 > 60

14. The product of two and x is greater than sixteen.

   a. x + 2 > 16
   b. x - 2 > 16
   c. 2x > 16
   d. x ÷ 2 > 16

15. The quotient when eighteen is divided by g is sixty-six.

   a. 18 + g = 66
   b. 18 - g = 66
   c. 18g = 66
   d. 18 ÷ g = 66

16. The sum of t and twenty is less than thirty-four.

    a. $t + 20 < 34$
    b. $t - 20 < 34$
    c. $t + 20 > 34$
    d. $t - 20 > 34$

17. Fifteen decreased by n is equal to eleven.

    a. $15 + n = 11$
    b. $15 - n = 11$
    c. $15n = 11$
    d. $15 \div n = 11$

18. Seventy-five times y is greater than one hundred fifty.

    a. $75y < 150$
    b. $75 \div y < 150$
    c. $75y > 150$
    d. $75 \div y > 150$

19. The sum of x and eight is less than fourteen.

    a. $x + 8 < 14$
    b. $x - 8 < 14$
    c. $x + 8 > 14$
    d. $x - 8 > 14$

20. The product of nineteen and k is greater than one hundred.

    a. $19k < 100$
    b. $19 \div k < 100$
    c. $19k > 100$
    d. $19 \div k > 100$

21. Thirty-six decreased by n is less than 5.

    a. $36 + n < 5$
    b. $36 - n < 5$
    c. $36 + n > 5$
    d. $36 - n > 5$

22. Forty-two divided by p is greater than seven.

    a. $p + 42 > 7$
    b. $p - 42 > 7$
    c. $42p > 7$
    d. $42 \div p > 7$

23. The difference between t and three is greater than twenty.

    a. $t - 3 > 20$
    b. $t - 3 < 20$
    c. $t + 3 < 20$
    d. $t + 3 > 20$

24. The quotient when w is divided by six is less than three.

    a. $w + 6 < 3$
    b. $w - 6 < 3$
    c. $6 \div w < 3$
    d. $w \div 6 < 3$

25. Forty greater than b is greater than one hundred.

    a. $b + 40 > 100$
    b. $b - 40 > 100$
    c. $40b > 100$
    d. $b \div 40 > 100$

Content Cluster – ALGEBRA AND FUNCTIONS (Evaluate Expressions)

Objective: Students will use the order of operations correctly to evaluate algebraic expressions.

> **Parent Tip:** When evaluating, replace all variables with their numerical value then do all the operations you can following the order of operations.
>
> **Note:** Two or more letters next to each other **or** a number and letters next to each other **means to multiply the values.** If a = 2 and b = 3 then 4ab = 4 x 2 x 3 = 24

For problems 1-6, evaluate each expression when x = 5 and y = 6

1. $xy + y$

    a. 30
    b. 60
    c. 62
    d. 36

2. $(y + x)x$

    a   31
    b. 55
    c. 35
    d. 16

3. $y(2x - y) + x$

    a. 15
    b. 29
    c. 44
    d. 54

4. $2x + y^2$

    a. 46
    b. 22
    c. 20
    d. 37

5. $(3x + 1) + 2y^2$

    a. 56
    b. 70
    c. 88
    d. 92

6. $xy^2 - 5$

    a. 151
    b. 795
    c. 895
    d. 175

For problems 7-12, evaluate each expression when a = 3, b = 4 and c = 9.

7. $3a^2b + 6c$

    a. 162
    b. 60
    c. 177
    d. 444

8. $5ab^2$

    a. 24
    b. 120
    c. 240
    d. 546

9. $\dfrac{c}{a^2} + b$

    a. 14
    b. 12
    c. 5
    d. 4

10. $\left(\dfrac{2b}{a}\right)(4a^2)$

    a. 96
    b. 72
    c. 30
    d. 13

11. $\dfrac{3c^2}{a} - b^2a$

    a. 7
    b. 21
    c. 33
    d. 57

12. $(2a + 2b)^2 - 4c$

    a. 85
    b. 160
    c. 232
    d. 260

Content Cluster –ALGEBRA AND FUNCTIONS(Simplify Expressions)

Objective: Students will simplify numerical expressions by applying properties of rational numbers (identity, inverse, distributive, associative, commutative).

Parent Tip: Before starting the problem, see if there are terms that work together to make the problem simpler and might be done mentally.

Examples:
$$\frac{1}{5} + \frac{12}{13} + \frac{^-1}{5} \rightarrow \left(\frac{1}{5} + \frac{^-1}{5}\right) + \frac{12}{13} \rightarrow 0 + \frac{12}{13} \rightarrow \frac{12}{13}$$

(group opposites)   **(use identity)**

$$\frac{1}{4} + 5\frac{1}{3} + \frac{3}{4} + \frac{2}{3} \rightarrow \left(5\frac{1}{3} + \frac{2}{3}\right) + \left(\frac{1}{4} + \frac{3}{4}\right) \rightarrow 6 + 1 = 7$$

(use commutative & associative)

$$8\left(\frac{^-7}{8} + \frac{5}{8} + \frac{^-1}{4}\right) \rightarrow 8\left(\frac{^-7}{8}\right) + 8\left(\frac{5}{8}\right) + 8\left(\frac{^-1}{4}\right) \rightarrow {^-7} + 5 + {^-2} = \left({^-7} + {^-2}\right) + 5 = {^-9} + 5 = {^-4}$$

(use distributive property)   **(use commutative & associative)**

Simplify each expression:

1. $\dfrac{3}{4} + \dfrac{1}{5} + \dfrac{1}{4}$ 2. $\dfrac{^-14}{18} + \dfrac{^-2}{9} - \dfrac{3}{18}$ 3. $\dfrac{8}{7}\left(\dfrac{^-14}{4} + \dfrac{21}{2}\right)$

a. $\dfrac{5}{13}$ a. $\dfrac{^-2}{3}$ a. 8

b. $1\dfrac{1}{5}$ b. $\dfrac{^-8}{9}$ b. $^-4$

c. $1\dfrac{1}{4}$ c. $^-1\dfrac{1}{6}$ c. 12

d. $\dfrac{5}{20}$ d. $^-1\dfrac{2}{3}$ d. 10

4. $\dfrac{^-3}{8} + \dfrac{1}{2}\left(\dfrac{^-7}{8} + \dfrac{7}{8}\right)$

    a. $\dfrac{1}{8}$

    b. $\dfrac{^-1}{8}$

    c. $\dfrac{^-3}{8}$

    d. $\dfrac{3}{8}$

5. $\dfrac{^-1}{2}\left(^-2 + 1\right)$

    a. 1

    b. $^-1$

    c. $\dfrac{1}{2}$

    d. $\dfrac{^-1}{2}$

6. $^-1\dfrac{1}{3} + 2\dfrac{1}{2} - \dfrac{2}{3} + 1\dfrac{1}{2}$

    a. 1

    b. 2

    c. $^-1$

    d. $^-2$

7. $2\dfrac{4}{5} - 3\dfrac{1}{2} + 1\dfrac{1}{5} - 4$

    a. $^-4$

    b. $3\dfrac{1}{2}$

    c. $^-3$

    d. $^-3\dfrac{1}{2}$

8. $2 - 3\dfrac{1}{3}\left(\dfrac{3}{10}\right) - \dfrac{^-1}{2}$

    a. $^-1\dfrac{1}{2}$

    b. $^-2$

    c. $1\dfrac{1}{2}$

    d. $2\dfrac{1}{2}$

Content Cluster – ALGEBRA AND FUNCTIONS
(AlgebraicTerminology)

Objective: Students will use algebraic terminology correctly, e.g. variable, equation, term, coefficient, inequality, expression, constant.

Parent Tip: Know the definitions:

Constant – something that is always the same: a number is a constant
Variable – a letter that represents a number of unknown value
Expression – a numerical or variable statement, no equal or inequality symbol
Term – the numbers or variables that are being added, subtracted, multiplied, etc
Coefficient – the number in front of the variable (2a, 5x, 1/3y)
Equation – a numerical or variable sentence that has an equal symbol (=)
Inequality - a numerical or variable sentence that has an inequality symbol (<,>)

Identify the underlined part:

1.   3 + <u>a</u> = 10

   a.   constant
   b.   variable
   c.   coefficient
   d.   equation

2.   <u>8</u>x - 4 = 20

   a.   constant
   b.   variable
   c.   coefficient
   d.   equation

3.   <u>5</u> + 3c > 18

   a.   constant
   b.   variable
   c.   coefficient
   d.   equation

4.   <u>2 + 10b = 42</u>

   a.   constant
   b.   term
   c.   inequality
   d.   equation

5.   <u>9d</u> + 14d + <u>8</u>

   a.   constant
   b.   variable
   c.   term
   d.   coefficient

6.   <u>13 + 80 + 6</u>

   a.   variable
   b.   coefficient
   c.   equation
   d.   expression

7.   2 + <u>0.5</u>f

   a.   term
   b.   coefficient
   c.   expression
   d.   equation

8.   <u>7g - 32 < 50</u>

   a.   term
   b.   expression
   c.   equation
   d.   inequality

9.   9<u>h</u> + 3<u>h</u> + 0.25<u>h</u>

   a.   variable
   b.   term
   c.   equation
   d.   expression

Content Cluster – ALGEBRA AND FUNCTIONS
(Graphical Interpretation)

Objective: Students will represent quantitative relationship graphically and interpret the meaning of a specific part of a graph in terms of the situation represented by the graph.

Parent Tip: Read the labels on the vertical and the horizontal lines of the graph to find out what is compared.

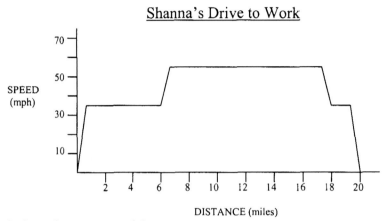

Shanna's Drive to Work

1. How far is it from home to work?

       a.   6 miles
       b.   15 miles
       c.   20 miles
       d.   not enough information

2. What type of road is driven from approximately mile 6.5 to mile17?

       a.   business streets
       b.   highways
       c.   residential streets
       d.   not enough information

3. Why is the graph upwardly steep between 0 and 0.5 miles and between 6 and 6.5 miles?

       a.   the car is accelerating
       b.   the car is slowing down
       c.   the car is on the highway
       d.   not enough information

4. Approximately how many miles of highway driving is there to work?

       a.   2 miles
       b.   5 miles
       c.   11 miles
       d.   not enough information

The graph below shows John's trip to the bike shop, a stop at his friend's house and back home.

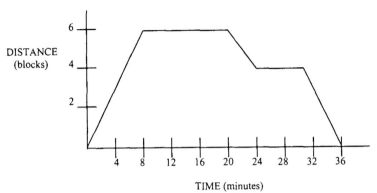

TIME (minutes)

5. How far is the bike shop from John's house?

   a.   4 blocks
   b.   6 blocks
   c.   8 blocks
   d.   not enough information

6. How long was John at the bike shop?

   a.   6 minutes
   b.   8 minutes
   c.   12 minutes
   d.   not enough information

7. How far is John's friend's house from John's house?

   a.   6 blocks
   b.   4 blocks
   c.   2 blocks
   d.   not enough information

8. How long was John at his friend's house?

   a.   3 minutes
   b.   5 minutes
   c.   7 minutes
   d.   not enough information

Content Cluster – ALGEBRA AND FUNCTIONS
(Positive/Negative Powers)

Objective: Students will interpret positive whole number as repeated multiplication and negative whole numbers as repeated division or multiplication by the multiplicative inverse. (Simplify and evaluate expressions that involve exponents.)

Parent Tip:

1) When a number is to a positive power, it means to take the number and multiply it by itself the same amount of times as the exponent valve.

$$\overset{\text{exponent}}{\downarrow}$$

Example: $\quad 2^4 = 2 \cdot 2 \cdot 2 \cdot 2 = 16$

$\qquad\qquad \underset{\text{base}}{\uparrow}$

2) When a number is to a negative power, invert the number [put the number in fraction form with 1 as the numerator (top) and the number as the denominator (bottom)]making the exponent positive.

Example: $\quad 2^{-4} = \dfrac{1}{2^4} = \dfrac{1}{2 \cdot 2 \cdot 2 \cdot 2} = \dfrac{1}{16}$

$\qquad\qquad\quad \underset{\uparrow}{}$

(the exponent becomes positive)

Simplify:

1. $3^2 + 2^2$
   - a. 6
   - b. 10
   - c. 13
   - d. 25

2. $5^2 - 2^4$
   - a. 9
   - b. 10
   - c. 3
   - d. 1

3. $4^{-2} + 3^{-2}$
   - a. $\dfrac{25}{144}$
   - b. $\dfrac{2}{25}$
   - c. 25
   - d. 49

4. $10^{-1} - 10^{-2}$
   - a. 9
   - b. 10
   - c. 0.09
   - d. 0.99

5. $6^2 - 2^{-3}$
   - a. 16
   - b. $35\dfrac{7}{8}$
   - c. $36\dfrac{1}{8}$
   - d. 64

6. $10^{-1} + 10^{-2} + 10^{-3}$
   - a. 111
   - b. 11.1
   - c. 1.11
   - d. 0.111

Parent Tip:

1) When multiplying with same bases, the rules for the exponents (negative/ positive) are the same – add the exponents for the new exponent value.

  Example: Positive Exponents → $\left(2^4\right)\left(2^4\right) = 2^{4+2} = 2^6 = 64$

  Negative Exponents → $\left(4^3\right)\left(4^{-1}\right) = 4^{3+^-1} = 4^2 = 16$

2) When dividing with the same bases, subtract the denominator (bottom number) exponent's value from the numerator (top number) exponent's value.

  Example: Positive Exponents → $\dfrac{3^6}{3^2} = 3^{6-2} = 3^4 = 81$

  Negative Exponents → $\dfrac{4^2}{4^{-1}} = 4^{2-^-1} = 4^3 = 64$

Simplify:

7. $\left(2^3\right)\left(2^{-4}\right)$

  a. 2
  b. 1
  c. $\dfrac{1}{2}$
  d. $\dfrac{1}{4}$

8. $\left(5^{-2}\right)\left(5^{-1}\right)$

  a. $\dfrac{1}{10}$
  b. $\dfrac{1}{25}$
  c. $\dfrac{1}{125}$
  d. $\dfrac{1}{625}$

9. $\dfrac{6^2}{6^{-2}}$

  a. 1296
  b. 216
  c. 36
  d. 6

10. $3^{-1} \div 3^2$

  a. 27
  b. 3
  c. $\dfrac{1}{9}$
  d. $\dfrac{1}{27}$

11. $\left(4^1\right)\left(4^{-2}\right)\left(4^3\right)$

  a. 4
  b. 16
  c. 64
  d. 256

12. $\dfrac{\left(10^{-1}\right)\left(10^{-3}\right)\left(10^6\right)}{10^2}$

  a. 0.01
  b. 0.1
  c. 1
  d. 10

Content Cluster – ALGEBRA AND FUNCTIONS (Monomials)

Objective: Students will be able to multiply and divide monomials.

Parent Tip: A monomial is a term in an expression, equation or inequality that is made up of numbers and letters **or** letters and letters.

Example: 3a, 4cd, abc, 63g

When multiplying or dividing monomials, multiply/divide the numbers by the numbers and the letters by the letters (**when same letters are being multiplied/divided, use exponents rules.**)

Example: $(6a)(2) = 6 \cdot 2 \cdot a = 12a$

$(10b)(3b) = 10 \cdot 3 \cdot b \cdot b = 30b^2$

$(8d)(4de) = 8 \cdot 4 \cdot d \cdot d \cdot e = 32d^2 e$

$\dfrac{20g^2}{4g} = \dfrac{20}{4} \cdot \dfrac{g \cdot g}{g} = 5g$

Simplify:

1. $(2a)(4a)$

    a. $8a$
    b. $2a^2$
    c. $4a^2$
    d. $8a^2$

2. $(6c)(7d)$

    a. $42cd$
    b. $40cd$
    c. $7cd$
    d. $6cd$

3. $4(2f)(3fg)$

    a. $24fg$
    b. $24f^2 g$
    c. $20fg$
    d. $20f^2 g$

4. $\dfrac{8abc}{2a}$

    a. $4bc$
    b. $4a^2 bc$
    c. $4abc$
    d. $4ab$

5. $\dfrac{64m^2 n^2}{4mn}$

    a. $16m^2 n$
    b. $16mn^2$
    c. $16mn$
    d. 16

6. $\dfrac{81r^3 s^4 t^2}{9rs^2 t^2}$

    a. $9r^2 s^2$
    b. $9r^2 s^2 t$
    c. $9rs^2 t^2$
    d. $9r^2 s^2 t^2$

7. $(10x^2 y^3 z^4)(10xyz)$

    a. $100xy^2 z^3$
    b. $100x^2 y^3 z^5$
    c. $100x^3 y^4 z^4$
    d. $100x^3 y^4 z^5$

8. $\dfrac{256pq}{16pq}$

    a. $16p$
    b. 16
    c. $16q$
    d. $16pq$

9. $\dfrac{4^3 \cdot 4^2 \cdot a^4 b^4 c^5}{4^5 \cdot a^4 b^4 c^5}$

    a. 0
    b. 1
    c. 2
    d. 4

Content Cluster – ALGEBRA AND FUNCTIONS (y = 2n)

Objective: Students will be able to graph functions in the form of
y = 2n and y = 3n and use in solving problems.

Parent Tip: When the function is in the form of y = 2n or y = 3n, it is in the direct variation form. When a value of n is replaced in the function, y will directly vary related to the constant value. The graph of this type of function will go through the origin (0,0) of the coordinate plane.

Example: $y = 15x$ $y = 3x \underline{+2}$ ← **can't** add or subtract from x
(Direct Variation Form)   (**NOT** Direct Variation Form)

Does y vary directly to x?

1. $y = 2x$

    a. yes
    b. no

2. $y = \dfrac{1}{2}x$

    a. yes
    b. no

3. $y = {}^-6x - 4$

    a. yes
    b. no

4. $y = 0.5x + 2$

    a. yes
    b. no

5. $y = {}^-3.75x$

    a. yes
    b. no

6. $y = {}^-\dfrac{4}{3}x - \dfrac{1}{9}$

    a. yes
    b. no

7. $x = 4y$

    a. yes
    b. no

8. $y = 2 + 4x$

    a. yes
    b. no

9. $y = {}^-\dfrac{7}{8}x + 0.875$

    a. yes
    b. no

CONTENT CLUSTER – Algebra and Functions (y = 2n)

Parent Tip: When graphing, the constant (number) determines how steep the graph is and if it is a positive slope (left-to-right up) or a negative slope (left-to-right up).

1) If the constant is **greater than 1**, the graph becomes **steeper**.
2) If the constant is **between 1 and 0**, the graph becomes **flatter**.
3) If the constant is **1**, the graph is at a **45° angle**.
4) If the constant is **positive**, the graph goes from **left-to-right up**.
5) If the constant is **negative**, the graph goes from **left-to-right down**.

Example: $y = 4x$ $y = \dfrac{^-1}{4}x$

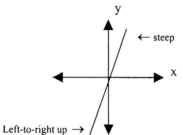

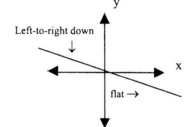

Which is the correct graph of the function given?

10. $y = 3x$

a.
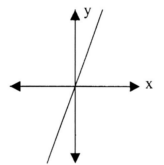

c.
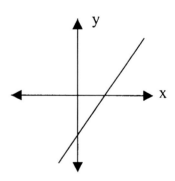

b.
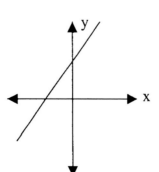

d.
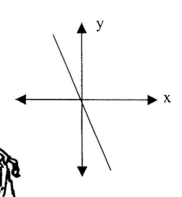

11. $y = \dfrac{^-1}{3}x$

a.

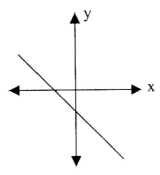

c.

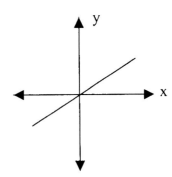

b.

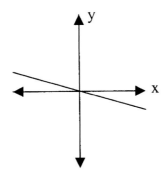

d.

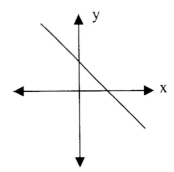

12. $y = 0.5x$

a.

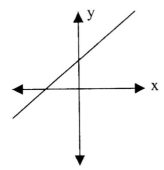

c.

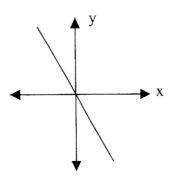

b.

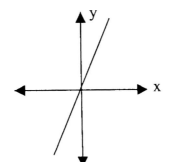

d.

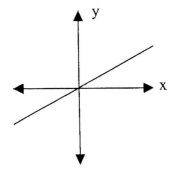

Content Cluster – ALGEBRA AND FUNCTIONS (Slope)

Objective: Students will graph linear functions, noting that the vertical change (change in the y-value) per unit of horizontal change (change in the x-value) is always the same and know that the ratio ("rise over run") is called the slope of the graph.

Parent Tip: When given two points on a graph, use the coordinates (x, y) of the two points to determine the slope. The difference between the x-coordinates represents the "run" (moving along the x-axis) and the difference between the y-coordinates represents the "rise" (up or down the y-axis).

Example: Point **A (2, 3)** and Point **B (6, 4)** are points on a graph. What is the slope ("rise over run") of the graph?

$$\text{Slope} = \frac{\text{rise}}{\text{run}} = \frac{(y_2 - y_1)}{(x_2 - x_1)} = \frac{(4 - 3)}{(6 - 2)} = \frac{1}{4}, \text{ the slope is } \frac{1}{4}$$

Note: x_1 and y_1 are the coordinates of the first point and

x_2 and y_2 are the coordinates of the second point

Find the slope of the graph from the given points on the graph:

1. P (4, 4) and Q (5, 5)

   a. $\dfrac{1}{5}$

   b. $\dfrac{1}{4}$

   c. 1

   d. 4

2. H (1, 3) and I (10, 7)

   a. $\dfrac{1}{2}$

   b. $\dfrac{10}{8}$

   c. $\dfrac{1}{4}$

   d. $\dfrac{4}{9}$

3. L (7, 8) and M (1, 2)

   a. $\dfrac{1}{4}$

   b. $\dfrac{1}{2}$

   c. $\dfrac{7}{8}$

   d. 1

4. N (3, 6) and O (5, 7)

   a. $\dfrac{1}{2}$

   b. $\dfrac{3}{7}$

   c. $\dfrac{5}{6}$

   d. $\dfrac{3}{5}$

5. C (1, 3) and D (4, 1)

   a. $\dfrac{^-1}{4}$

   b. $\dfrac{^-1}{3}$

   c. $\dfrac{^-3}{4}$

   d. $\dfrac{^-2}{3}$

6. E (10, 7) and F (8, 6)

   a. $\dfrac{2}{3}$

   b. $\dfrac{1}{2}$

   c. $\dfrac{^-2}{3}$

   d. $\dfrac{^-1}{2}$

Parent Tip: If you know the slope of a graph, you can choose any point on the graph and go up (or down) the value of the numerator from that point then over (right or left) the value of the denominator, you will be back on the graph.

Example: The slope is $\frac{2}{3}$ and the point is (2, 4). Is the point (5, 6) on the graph?

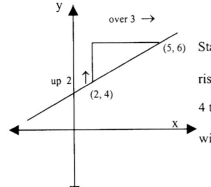

Start at (2, 4) and since the slope is $\frac{2}{3}$ (2 represents the rise and the 3 represents the run) **add** 2 to the y-coordinate 4 to get **6** and 3 to the x-coordinate to get **5**. The point (5, 6) will be on the graph.

What other point is on the graph?

7. Slope = 1 $\left(\frac{1}{1}\right)$, A (3, 4)

   a. (4, 5)
   b. (4, 6)
   c. (5, 5)
   d. (5, 6)

8. Slope = $\frac{^-1}{2}$, B (9, 10)

   a. (9, 12)
   b. (11, 11)
   c. (10, 12)
   d. (11, 9)

9. Slope = $\frac{7}{8}$, C $\left(^-4, ^-5\right)$

   a. $\left(^-4, ^-2\right)$
   b. $\left(4, ^-2\right)$
   c. $\left(^-4, 2\right)$
   d. $(4, 2)$

10. Slope = $\frac{^-7}{3}$, D $\left(^-3, 7\right)$

   a. (0, 0)
   b. (6, 0)
   c. (0, 7)
   d. $\left(^-6, ^-14\right)$

Content Cluster –ALGEBRA AND FUNCTIONS (Two-Step Equations)

Objective: Students will solve two-step linear equations and inequalities in one variable over the rational numbers.

Parent Tip: When solving a two-step linear equation, or inequality, reverse the order of operations. Undo the addition/subtraction first then undo the multiplication/division next.

$$\text{Example:} \qquad \frac{1}{2}x + \frac{1}{4} = \frac{3}{4}$$

$$-\frac{1}{4} \quad -\frac{1}{4} \qquad \leftarrow \text{Subtract } \frac{1}{4} \text{ from both sides}$$

$$\frac{1}{2}x + 0 = \frac{2}{4}$$

$$\frac{1}{2}x = \frac{1}{2}$$

$$(2)\frac{1}{2}x = \frac{1}{2}(2) \qquad \leftarrow \text{Multiply both sides by 2 (reciprocal of } \frac{1}{2})$$

$$x = 1$$

Note: The procedure for inequalities is the same, except when multiplying or dividing by a negative value, the inequality symbol reverses.

Solve:

1. $\frac{1}{2}x + \frac{1}{8} = \frac{3}{4}$

     a. $\frac{1}{4}$

     b. $\frac{1}{2}$

     c. $\frac{5}{4}$

     d. $\frac{3}{2}$

2. $\frac{1}{3}y - \frac{1}{2} = \frac{2}{3}$

     a. 3

     b. $\frac{7}{2}$

     c. 4

     d. $\frac{9}{2}$

3. $\frac{3}{8}b + \frac{1}{4} = \frac{7}{8}$

     a. $\frac{4}{3}$

     b. $\frac{5}{3}$

     c. 2

     d. $\frac{7}{3}$

CONTENT CLUSTER – Algebra and Functions (Two-Step Equations)

4. $\dfrac{2}{9} + \dfrac{5}{6}n < \dfrac{8}{9}$

    a. $n < \dfrac{1}{3}$

    b. $n < \dfrac{2}{3}$

    c. $n < 1$

    d. $n < \dfrac{4}{5}$

5. $\dfrac{1}{4}p - \dfrac{1}{3} = \dfrac{1}{2}$

    a. $\dfrac{7}{3}$

    b. $\dfrac{8}{3}$

    c. 3

    d. $\dfrac{10}{3}$

6. $\dfrac{1}{4}y + \dfrac{1}{8} > \dfrac{15}{16}$

    a. $y > \dfrac{13}{4}$

    b. $y > \dfrac{17}{4}$

    c. $y > \dfrac{19}{4}$

    d. $y > \dfrac{9}{16}$

7. $\dfrac{^-1}{8}d - \dfrac{1}{4} = \dfrac{1}{2}$

    a. $^-4$

    b. $^-5$

    c. $^-6$

    d. $^-7$

8. $1\dfrac{1}{2} - \dfrac{1}{10}g = 3$

    a. $^-15$

    b. $^-14$

    c. $^-13$

    d. $^-12$

9. $^-3\dfrac{1}{3}h - \dfrac{1}{6} = 4$

    a. $\dfrac{^-7}{4}$

    b. $\dfrac{7}{4}$

    c. $\dfrac{^-5}{4}$

    d. $\dfrac{5}{4}$

Content Cluster–ALGEBRA AND FUNCTIONS (Multi-Step Problems)

Objective: Students will solve multi-step problems involving rate, average speed, distance and time, or direct variation.

Parent Tip: the definitions and formulas are important to remember for this concept

Rate → the comparison of <u>two</u> different units of measure, e.g. $^{cost}/_{gal}$, $^{miles}/_{hour}$

Distance = rate x times
         (speed) (hours)

Direct variation → $y = 4x$, y varies directly to the value of **x**

---

1. A car is traveling at 35 miles per hour (mph), How far will the car travel in $3 \frac{1}{2}$ hours?

    a. $122 \frac{1}{2}$ miles   c. 70 miles

    b. $105 \frac{1}{2}$ miles   d. 80miles

2. Bananas cost \$1.15/pound, apples \$0.79/pound and grapes \$1.29/pound. How much would it cost to buy 2 pounds of bananas, 3 pounds of apples and 1 pound of grapes?

    a. \$2.30   c. \$4.67
    b. \$2.37   d. \$5.96

3. Hanna drove 480 miles in $10 \frac{2}{3}$ hours. What rate was she traveling?

    a. 43 mph   c. 47 mph
    b. 45 mph   d. 50 mph

4. Find the perimeter of a rectangle if the length is 3 times the width and the width is 5 inches.

    a. 20 inches   c. 30 inches
    b. 25 inches   d. 40 inches

5. Gas cost $1.55/gal. How many gallons of gas can you buy for $20.00?

    a.   12.0 gallons   c.   12.9 gallons
    b.   12.5 gallons   d.   13.9 gallons

6. An isosceles triangle has a base that is 2 times the length of one of the other sides. If the base is 6 centimeters long, find the perimeter of the triangle.

    a.   12 centimeters   c.   6 centimeters
    b.   9 centimeters   d.   3 centimeters

Content Cluster – MEASUREMENT AND GEOMETRY
(Compare Measurements)

Objective: Students will compare weights, capacities, geometric measures, times and temperatures within and between measurement systems (cubic inches to cubic cm).

Parent Tip: There are certain conversions that need to be familiar:

<table>
<tr><td>

Length

12 inches (in) = 1 foot (ft)
3 feet = 1 yard (yd)
5280 feet = 1 mile (mi)
1760 yards = 1 mile

</td><td>

Weight

16 ounces (oz) = 1 pound (lb)
2000 pounds = 1 ton (T)

</td></tr>
<tr><td>

Capacity

8 fluid ounces (fl oz) = 1 cup (c)
2 cups = 1 pint (pt)
2 pint = 1 quarter (qt)
4 quarters = 1 gallon (gal)

</td><td>

Time

60 seconds (sec) = 1 minute (min)
60 minutes = 1 hour (hr)
24 hours = 1 day
7 days = 1 week (wk)
52 weeks = 1 year (yr)
365 days = 1 year

</td></tr>
</table>

Convert the following measurements:

1. 5 miles = _?_ yards

   a. 8800
   b. 7800
   c. 6800
   d. 7040

2. 1 gallon = _?_ cups

   a. 4
   b. 8
   c. 16
   d. 32

3. 1 day = _?_ minutes

   a. 180
   b. 360
   c. 720
   d. 1440

4. 1 ton = _?_ ounces

   a. 32,000
   b. 16,000
   c. 8,000
   d. 2,000

5. 1 week = _?_ hours

   a. 168
   b. 144
   c. 120
   d. 60

6. 1 year = _?_ hours

   a. 7760
   b. 8760
   c. 3600
   d. 2000

CONTENT CLUSTER – Measurement and Geometry (Compare Measurements)

Parent Tip: Converting from one system to another, be familiar with the base conversions.

Standard System		Metric System
1 inch	→	2.54 centimeters
1 yard	→	39 centimeters
1 pound	→	454 grams
2.2 pounds	→	1 kilogram
1 square inch (in^2)	→	6.45 square centimeters (cm^2)
1 cubic inch (in^3)	→	16.39 cubic centimeters (cm^3)

7. 3 pounds = ? grams

    a. 151
    b. 454
    c. 1362
    d. 1816

8. 25.4 cm = ? in

    a. 4
    b. 6
    c. 8
    d. 10

9. 10 kg = ? pounds

    a. 22
    b. 20
    c. 18
    d. 16

10. 2497 g = ? pounds

    a. 4.75
    b. 5.00
    c. 5.25
    d. 5.50

11. 273 inches = ? meters

    a. 6
    b. 7
    c. 8
    d. 8.5

12. 4 in^2 = ? cm^2

    a. 20.8
    b. 25.8
    c. 30.8
    d. 35.8

13. 10 in^3 = ? cm^3

    a. 163.9
    b. 144
    c. 327.8
    d. 1728

14. 161.25 cm^2 = ? in^2

    a. 22
    b. 23
    c. 24
    d. 25

15. 1639 cm^3 = ? in^3

    a. 1
    b. 10
    c. 100
    d. 1000

Content Cluster – MEASUREMENT AND GEOMETRY
(Perimeter, Area, Volume)

Objective: Students will use formulas for finding the perimeter and area of basic two-dimensional figures and for finding surface area and volume of basic three-dimensional figures.

Before starting this cluster, it is important to review some of the definitions and formulas that need to be used to be successful:

Definitions:

Perimeter of a polygon – the distance around the figure, in other words, add up all the measurements of the sides.

Area of a polygon – the number of square units inside the polygon.

Formulas:

Area of a Triangle – $A = \dfrac{b \cdot h}{2}$

Area of a Square – $A = b \cdot h$

Area of a Rhombus – $A = b \cdot h$

Area of a Trapezoid – $A = \dfrac{(b_1 + b_2)\, h}{2}$

Area of a Circle – $A = \pi \cdot r^2$

Area of a Rectangle – $A = b \cdot h$

Area of a Parallelogram – $A = b \cdot h$

Circumference of a Circle – $C = \pi \cdot d$

Use the following figure to answer questions 1-2:

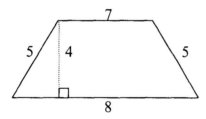

1. Find the perimeter of the figure.

   a. 14   c. 25
   b. 24   d. 29

2. Find the area of the figure.

   a. 20   c. 40
   b. 30   d. 50

Use the following figure to answer questions 3-4:

3. Find the perimeter of the figure.

   a. 20   c. 16.5
   b. 19.5   d. 14.5

4. Find the area of the figure.

   a. 28   c. 15.75
   b. 12.75   d. 31.5

Use the following figure to answer questions 5-6:

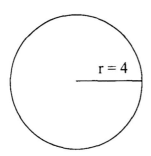

5. Find the circumference of the circle.
    (use $\pi = 3.14$)

    a. 6.28   c. 25.12
    b. 12.56   d. 50.24

6. Find the area of the figure.
    (use $\pi = 3.14$)

    a. 6.28   c. 25.12
    b. 12.56   d. 50.24

Use the following figure to answer questions 7-8:

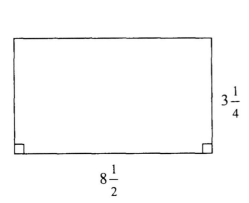

7. Find the perimeter of the figure.

    a. $23\frac{1}{2}$ c. $18\frac{3}{4}$

    b. $22\frac{1}{2}$ d. $16\frac{3}{4}$

8. Find the area of the figure.

    a. $24\frac{1}{8}$ c. $27\frac{5}{8}$

    b. $24\frac{3}{4}$ d. $27\frac{7}{8}$

Parent Tip: When we working with solid shapes, they are **prisms** and **pyramids**.
Prism – a three-dimensional figure that has two bases.

Pyramid – a three-dimensional figure with one base.

Definitions:

Base – the polygons in a prism that are the same shape opposite each other.
Their bases name prisms and pyramids, i.e. a **triangular prism** has 2 triangle bases.

Height – the height of a prism is the distance between the 2 bases and the height of a pyramid is the distance between point and the base.

Volume – the volume of a solid figure is the number of cubic units inside.

Formulas:

Volume of a Prism – $V = Bh$ (B = the base area)

Volume of a Pyramid – $V = \dfrac{1}{3} Bh$ (B = the base area)

Base Area – the area of the base. Use the area formulas for polygons to get the base area.

9. Find the volume.

   a.   9
   b. 18
   c. 27
   d. 36

10. Find the volume.(use $\pi = 3.14$)

   a. 16
   b. 25.12
   c. 41.12
   d. 50.24

11. Find the volume.

   a.   20
   b.   30
   c.   60
   d. 120

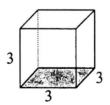

12. Find the volume.

   a. 20
   b. 25
   c. 50
   d. 75

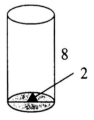

13. Find the volume. (use $\pi = 3.14$)

    a.   56.52
    b.   28.26
    c.   14.13
    d.   3.14

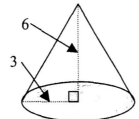

14. Find the volume. ($\mathbf{B} = 20$)

    a.   80
    b.   90
    c.   100
    d.   120

Parent Tip: When working with **surface area**, you need to find <u>all</u> the areas of <u>all</u> the faces (flat surfaces) of the prism. The area formulas are used so make sure you revisit them.

Example:

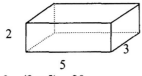

2 x (2 x 5) = 20
2 x (2 x 3) = 12
+ 2 x (3 x 5) = 30
         62

There are **two** faces **2 x 5** –
(front and back)

There are **two** faces **2 x 3** –
(the two sides)

There are **two** faces **3 x 5** –
(top and bottom)

---

15. Find the surface area.

    a.   82
    b.   128
    c.   164
    d.   216

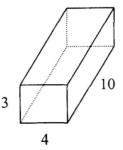

16. Find the surface area.

    a.   216
    b.   240
    c.   360
    d.   400

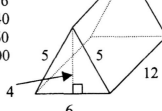

Content Cluster – MEASUREMENT AND GEOMETRY
(Complex Figures)

Objective: Students will estimate and compute the area of more complex or irregular two-dimensional figures.

Parent Tip: If you are working with unusual geometric shapes, break them into commonly known shapes.

Example:

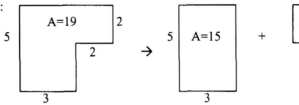

To find the area of the figure, divide the figure into two rectangles, find their areas and add them together.

Definitions:

Area of a polygon – the number of square units inside the polygon.

Formulas:

Area of a Triangle – $A = \dfrac{b \cdot h}{2}$

Area of a Square – $A = b \cdot h$

Area of a Rhombus – $A = b \cdot h$

Area of a Trapezoid – $A = \dfrac{(b_1 + b_2)\, h}{2}$

Area of a Circle – $A = \pi \cdot r^2$

Area of a Rectangle – $A = b \cdot h$

Area of a Parallelogram – $A = b \cdot h$

Circumference of a Circle – $C = \pi \cdot d$

Find the area of the following figures.

1.

3.5

3.5

3.5

   a. 24.25
   b. 26.75
   c. 36.75
   d. 40.25

2.

6

3

6

   a. 25
   b. 27
   c. 36
   d. 40

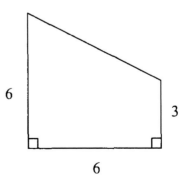

Find the area of the following figures.

3.

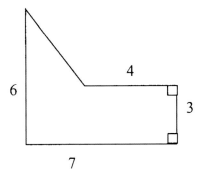

6

4

3

7

   a. 25.5
   b. 26.5
   c. 36.5
   d. 40.5

4.

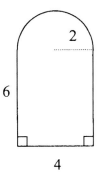

2

6

4

(use $\pi = 3.14$)
   a. 24.28
   b. 26.28
   c. 36.56
   d. 40.56

5.

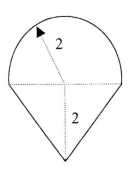

2

2

(use $\pi = 3.14$)
   a. 3.14
   b. 6.28
   c. 8.28
   d. 10.28

6.

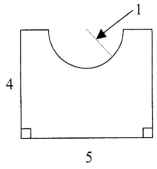

1

4

5

(use $\pi = 3.14$)
   a. 18.43
   b. 20.43
   c. 23.14
   d. 24.14

Content Cluster – MEASUREMENT AND GEOMETRY (Scale Factor)

Objective: Students will compute the length of the perimeter, the surface area of the faces and the volume of a three-dimensional object built from rectangular solids. They will understand that the lengths of all dimensions are multiplied by a scale factor, the surface area is multiplied by the square of the scale factor and the volume is multiplied by the cube of the scale factor.

Parent Tip: The scale factor is the number of times the figure is increased.

Example:

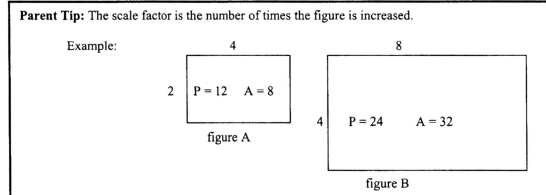

figure A

figure B

Figure B is 2 times larger than figure A, the perimeter of figure B will be **2 times** larger than figure A (perimeter is length) but the area of figure B is **4 times** larger than figure A (area is in square units).

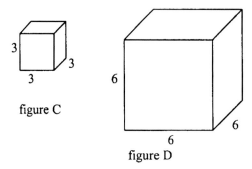

figure C

figure D

Figure D is 2 times larger than figure C, the volume of figure D will be **8 times** larger than figure C (volume is in cubic units). Volume of figure C is **27** cubic units and the volume of figure D is **216** cubic units (27 x 8 = 216).

Use the figures below to answer questions 1 – 6:

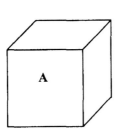
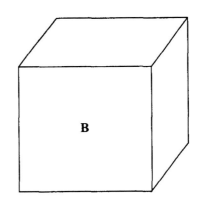

The edges of cube A are 4 cm each.
Cube B is twice as large as cube A.

1. What is the perimeter of <u>one</u> face of cube A?

 a. 8
 b. 16
 c. 24
 d. 32

2. What is the perimeter of <u>one</u> face of cube B?

 a. 32
 b. 64
 c. 96
 d. 100

3. What is the area of <u>one</u> face of cube A?

 a. 4
 b. 6
 c. 8
 d. 16

4. What is the area of <u>one</u> face of cube B?

 a. 32
 b. 64
 c. 96
 d. 100

5. What is the volume of cube A?

 a. 32
 b. 64
 c. 96
 d. 100

6. What is the volume of cube B?

 a. 64
 b. 128
 c. 256
 d. 512

Content Cluster – MEASUREMENT AND GEOMETRY
(Change Measurement)

Objective: Students will relate the change in measurement under change of scale to the units used (square inches, cubic feet) and to the conversions between units (1 square foot = 144 square inches).

Parent Tip: When using square units or cubic units, first multiply the conversion factor by itself (3 feet = 1 yard → 3 x 3 = 9, giving you 9 square feet = 1 square yard) and then multiply by the number of units given.

Example:

12 square yards = _?_ square feet

First, convert the unit values: (1 yd = 3 ft), therefore

$$1 \text{ yd} \times 1 \text{ yd} = 3 \text{ ft} \times 3 \text{ ft}$$
$$1 \text{ yd}^2 = \mathbf{9} \text{ ft}^2$$

Second, multiply the new unit value by the amount given:

$$9 \text{ ft}^2 \times \mathbf{12} = 108 \text{ ft}^2$$

Answer – 108 ft^2

(The same procedure is used with cubic units except multiply the conversion value by **itself** three (3) times.)

Standard System Conversions

1 square foot (ft^2) = 144 square inches (in^2)

1 square yard (yd^2) = 9 square feet (ft^2)

1 cubic foot (ft^3) = 1728 cubic inches (in^3)

1 cubic yard (yd^3) = 27 cubic feet (ft^3)

Find the Values:

1. $4 \text{ ft}^2 = $ _?_ in^2

   a. 288 in^2
   b. 576 in^2
   c. 144 in^2
   d. 432 in^2

2. $7 \text{ ft}^3 = $ _?_ in^3

   a. 84 in^3
   b. 288 in^3
   c. 11,096 in^3
   d. 12,096 in^3

3. $10 \text{ yd}^2 = $ _?_ ft^2

   a. 90 ft^2
   b. 900 ft^2
   c. 30 ft^2
   d. 300 ft^2

4. $14,400 \text{ in}^2 = $ _?_ ft^2

   a. 10 ft^2
   b. 20 ft^2
   c. 100 ft^2
   d. 200 ft^2

5. $81 \text{ ft}^3 = $ _?_ yd^3

   a. 3 yd^3
   b. 4 yd^3
   c. 5 yd^3
   d. 6 yd^3

6. $12 \text{ yd}^2 = $ _?_ in^2

   a. 14,552 in^2
   b. 15,552 in^2
   c. 572 in^2
   d. 672 in^2

Parent Tip: The metric system is based on groupings of tens (10), e.g. 10 millimeters = 1 centimeter, 10 centimeters = 1 decimeter, 10 decimeters = 1 meter, and so on. The prefixes will tell you the amount of or the part of the metric unit you have and if you know the units of measure – **meter** (length), **gram** (weight) and **liter** (capacity) – and the meaning of the prefixes, the metric system and its conversion become easier.

<u>Units of Measurement</u> – **Meter** (length), **Gram** (weight) and **Liter** (capacity)

<u>Prefixes and Meanings</u> –
        Parts of the Unit – **milli-** a thousandth (0.001) of the unit
                         centi- a hundredth (0.01) of the unit
                         deci- a tenth (0.1) of the unit
        Amount of Units – **deka-** ten (10) of the units
                         hecto- hundred (100) of the units
                         kilo- thousand (1000) of the units

        Examples: 4 hectometers = 400 meters, 5 kilograms = 5000 grams
                      3 milliliters = 0.003 liters, 7 decimeters = 0.7 meters

Find the Values:

7. 100 centimeters = _?_ meters

    a. 100 meters
    b. 10 meters
    c. 1 meters
    d. 0.1 meters

8. 2 kilograms = _?_ grams

    a. 20,000 grams
    b. 2,000 grams
    c. 200 grams
    d. 20 grams

9. 35 milliliters = _?_ liters

    a. 0.035 liters
    b. 0.35 liters
    c. 3.5 liters
    d. 35 liters

10. 575 meters = _?_ kilometers

    a. 575 kilometers
    b. 57.5 kilometers
    c. 5.75 kilometers
    d. 0.575 kilometers

11. 2,500 liters = _?_ kiloliters

    a. 0.025 liters
    b. 0.25 liters
    c. 2.5 liters
    d. 25 liters

12. 50 milligrams = _?_ grams

    a. 0.05 grams
    b. 0.5 grams
    c. 5 grams
    d. 50 grams

Parent Tip: When using square units or cubic units, first multiply the conversion factor by itself (10 decimeters = 1 meter → 10 x 10 = 100, giving you 100 square decimeters = 1 square meter) and then multiply by the number of units given.

Example:

12 square meters = _?_ square centimeters

First, convert the unit values: (100 cm = 1 m), therefore

1 m x 1 m = 100 cm x 100 cm

$1 \ m^2 = \mathbf{10,000} \ cm^2$

Second, multiply the new unit value by the amount given:

$10,000 \ m^2 \ x \ \mathbf{12} = 120,000 \ cm^2$

Answer – 120,000 cm^2

(The same procedure is used with cubic units except multiply the conversion value by **itself** three (3) times.)

Find the Values:

13. $4 \ m^2 = \underline{\ ? \ } mm^2$

    a.   4,000 mm^2
    b.   40,000 mm^2
    c.   400,000 mm^2
    d. 4,000,000 mm^2

14. $200 \ dm^2 = \underline{\ ? \ } m^2$

    a.   2 m^2
    b.   3 m^2
    c.   4 m^2
    d.   20 m^2

15. $25 \ hm^2 = \underline{\ ? \ } km^2$

    a.   25 km^2
    b. 0.025 km^2
    c. 0.25 km^2
    d.   2.5 km^2

16. $4 \ cm^3 = \underline{\ ? \ } mm^3$

    a.   40 mm^3
    b.   400 mm^3
    c. 4,000 mm^3
    d. 40,000 mm^3

17. $5 \ km^3 = \underline{\ ? \ } m^3$

    a.   50,000 m^3
    b.   500,000 m^3
    c. 5,000,000 m^3
    d. 50,000,000 m^3

18. $1 \ km^2 = \underline{\ ? \ } mm^2$

    a.   10,000,000,000 mm^2
    b.   100,000,000,000 mm^2
    c. 1,000,000,000,000 mm^2
    d. 10,000,000,000,000 mm^2

Content Cluster – MEASUREMENT AND GEOMETRY
(Coordinate Graph)

Objective: Students will understand and use coordinate graphs to plot simple figures, determine lengths and areas related to them, and determine their image under translation and reflection.

Parent Tip: When using figures on a coordinate graph (x- and y-axis):

1) Make sure that the figure has a right angle in it so you know the base and the height (the <u>two</u> sides that form the right angle are the base and the height).

2) To find the length of **the base**, subtract the x-coordinates and to find the length of **the height**, subtract the y-coordinates.

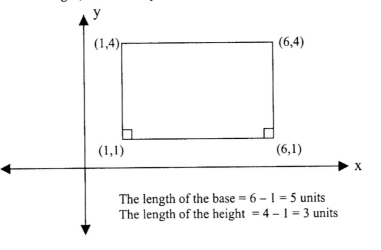

The length of the base = 6 – 1 = 5 units
The length of the height = 4 – 1 = 3 units

Knowing the base and the height, the perimeter (5 + 3 + 5 + 3 = 16) and the area (5 x 3 = 15) can be found.

Use the adjacent figure for problems 1 and 2:

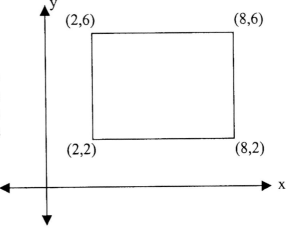

1. Find the perimeter.

   a. 10 units
   b. 14 units
   c. 20 units
   d. 24 units

2. Find the area.

   a. 24 square units
   b. 28 square units
   c. 32 square units
   d. 36 square units

Use the adjacent figure for problems 3 and 4:

3. Find the perimeter.

    a. 15 units
    b. 20 units
    c. 25 units
    d. 30 units

4. Find the area.

    a. 15 square units
    b. 20 square units
    c. 25 square units
    d. 30 square units

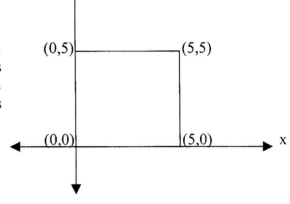

Use the adjacent figure for problems 5 and 6:

5. Find the perimeter.
    (**Hint:** use Pythagorean Theorem)

    a. 20 units
    b. 24 units
    c. 36 units
    d. 48 units

6. Find the area.

    a. 192 square units
    b. 174 square units
    c. 168 square units
    d. 244 square units

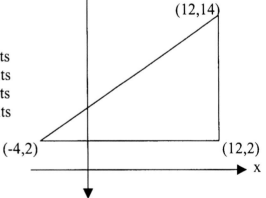

Parent Tip: The reflection of an image is to reverse the image and put it on the other side of a given line, same distance from the line.

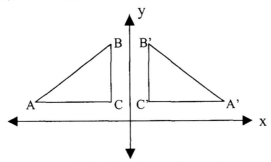

△ABC is reflected over the y-axis.

The translation of an image is to move it to a new location on the graph without changing its shape, size or direction.

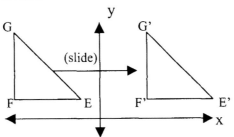

△EFG is translated to a new location.

How is the image being moved?

7.

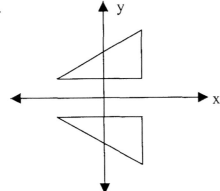

   a.   reflection
   b.   translation

8.

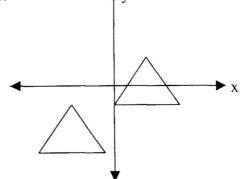

   a.   reflection
   b.   translation

How is the image being moved?

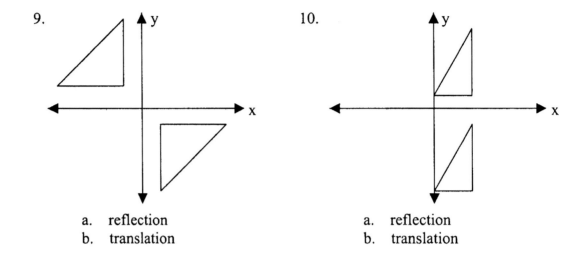

9.

a. reflection
b. translation

10.

a. reflection
b. translation

Content Cluster – MEASUREMENT AND GEOMETRY
(Pythagorean Theorem)

Objective: Students will know and understand the Pythagorean Theorem and use it to find the length of missing sides of right triangles and length of the other line segments.

Parent Tip:

The Pythagorean Theorem is:

$$a^2 + b^2 = c^2$$

altitude   base   hypotenuse

Find the length of the hypotenuse if the lengths of the sides are 3 and 4.

$a = 3$, $b = 4$ and $c = ?$

$$c^2 = a^2 + b^2$$
$$c^2 = 3^2 + 4^2$$
$$c^2 = 9 + 16$$
$$c^2 = 25$$
$$\sqrt{c^2} = \sqrt{25}$$
$$c = 5$$

Find the length of the missing side if the hypotenuse is 13 and the other side is 12.

$c = 13$, $a = 12$ and $b = ?$

$$c^2 = a^2 + b^2$$
$$13^2 = 12^2 + b^2$$
$$169 = 144 + b^2$$
$$\underline{-144 \quad -144}$$
$$25 = b^2$$
$$\sqrt{25} = \sqrt{b^2}$$
$$5 = b$$

Find the length of the missing side of the right triangle:
(Round your answer to the nearest tenth)

1. $a = 5$, $b = 6$, $c = \underline{\ ?\ }$

    a. 6.8
    b. 7.2
    c. 7.8
    d. 8.1

2. $a = 3$, $b = 5$, $c = \underline{\ ?\ }$

    a. 5.4
    b. 5.8
    c. 6.2
    d. 6.6

3. $a = 10$, $b = 14$, $c = \underline{\ ?\ }$

    a. 16.4
    b. 16.8
    c. 17.2
    d. 17.5

4. $c = 16$, $b = 9$, $a = \underline{\ ?\ }$

    a. 13.2
    b. 13.8
    c. 14.6
    d. 14.9

5. $c = 40$, $b = 27$, $a = \underline{\ ?\ }$

    a. 28.0
    b. 28.5
    c. 29.0
    d. 29.5

6. $c = 9$, $a = 3$, $b = \underline{\ ?\ }$

    a. 8.5
    b. 9.0
    c. 9.5
    d. 10.0

CONTENT CLUSTER – Measurement and Geometry (Pythagorean Theorem)

Find the length of the missing side of the right triangle:
(Round your answer to the nearest tenth)

7. $b = 18, a = 11, c = \underline{?}$

    a. 19.1
    b. 20.5
    c. 21.1
    d. 22.5

8. $b = 40, a = 50, c = \underline{?}$

    a. 49.0
    b. 64.0
    c. 81.0
    d. 100.0

9. $b = 120, a = 90, c = \underline{?}$

    a. 120.0
    b. 130.0
    c. 140.0
    d. 150.0

Content Cluster – MEASUREMENT AND GEOMETRY (Congruency)

Objective: Students will understand when two geometrical figures are congruent and what congruence means between the sides and angles.

Parent Tip: Congruent figures are figures that have the same size corresponding angles and the ratios of the corresponding sides are the same.

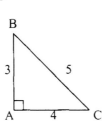 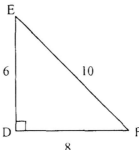

Given: $\angle A = \angle D$; $\angle B = \angle E$; $\angle C = \angle F$

$$\frac{AB}{DE} = \frac{3}{6} = \frac{1}{2}; \quad \frac{BC}{EF} = \frac{5}{10} = \frac{1}{2}; \quad \frac{AC}{DF} = \frac{4}{8} = \frac{1}{2}$$

(the ratios of the corresponding sides are the same)

then $\triangle ABC \cong \triangle DEF$

Since the ratio is 1:2 $\left(\dfrac{1}{2}\right)$ and <u>one</u> of the sides was unknown, to solve for the missing side just double the corresponding side to get the larger length <u>or</u> divide the corresponding side by 2 to get the smaller length.

Use the adjacent figure to solve for the missing side or angle:

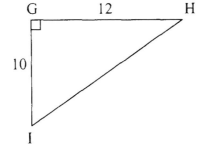 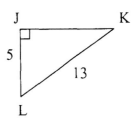

Given:
$\angle G = \angle J$
$\angle I = \angle L$

1. $\angle H = \underline{\ ?\ }$

    a. $\angle L$
    b. $\angle K$
    c. $\angle I$
    d. $\angle G$

2. $JK = \underline{\ ?\ }$

    a. 24
    b. 15
    c. 6
    d. 5

3. $HI = \underline{\ ?\ }$

    a. 26
    b. 24
    c. 20
    d. 15

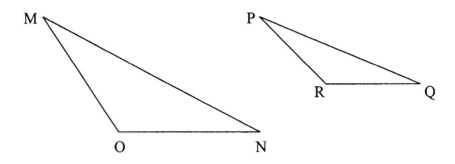

$\triangle MNO \cong \triangle PQR, \quad MN = 30, \quad PQ = 10$

4. $\angle O = \underline{?}$

    a. $\angle P$
    b. $\angle Q$
    c. $\angle R$
    d. $\angle N$

5. $\angle N = \underline{?}$

    a. $\angle P$
    b. $\angle Q$
    c. $\angle R$
    d. $\angle O$

6. If $RP = 8$, then $MO = \underline{?}$

    a. 4
    b. 8
    c. 16
    d. 24

7. If $MN = 42$, then $PQ = \underline{?}$

    a. 7
    b. 10
    c. 14
    d. 15

8. If $\angle O = 120°$, then $\angle R = \underline{?}$

    a. 120°
    b. 110°
    c. 100°
    d. 90°

9. If $\angle P = 37°$, then $\angle M = \underline{?}$

    a. 153°
    b. 143°
    c. 53°
    d. 37°

(Remember: All squares and equilateral triangles are **congruent**.)

Objective: Students will identity elements of three-dimensional objects (diagonals, skew lines, 3 ways planes intersect)

Parent Tip: Definitions used when working with three-dimensional figures.

Face – the flat surface of a three-dimensional figure
Edge – where two faces meet
Vertex (plural: vertices) – where three or more edges meet (the corners)
Diagonal – a line that connects two non-adjacent vertices
Skew Line – two lines that do not intersect and are not parallel

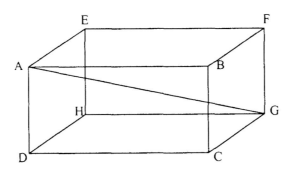

Faces – ABCD, EFGH, BCGF, ADHE, CDHG, ABFE
Vertices – A, B, C, D, E, F, G, H
Edges - $\overline{AB}$, $\overline{AE}$, $\overline{EF}$, $\overline{BF}$, $\overline{AD}$, $\overline{BC}$, $\overline{FG}$, $\overline{EH}$, $\overline{DC}$, $\overline{CG}$, $\overline{GH}$, $\overline{DH}$

Diagonals - $\overline{AG}$

Skew Lines - $\overline{AD} = \overline{HG}$, $\overline{EF} = \overline{BC}$ are some of the skew lines

---

Use the adjacent figure to determine questions:

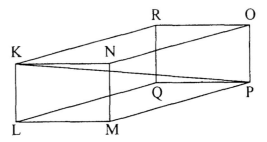

1. a face

   a. KROP
   b. MNOP
   c. MNRQ
   d. LQPO

2. a vertex

   a. $\overline{KN}$
   b. MQ
   c. Q
   d. KLMN

3. an edge

   a. $\overline{KN}$
   b. $\overline{KP}$
   c. Q
   d. KLMN

4. a diagonal

   a. $\overline{KN}$
   b. $\overline{KR}$
   c. $\overline{KL}$
   d. $\overline{KP}$

5. skew lines

   a. $\overline{KN}$ and $\overline{RO}$
   b. $\overline{RQ}$ and $\overline{QP}$
   c. $\overline{KL}$ and $\overline{PQ}$
   d. $\overline{LQ}$ and $\overline{MP}$

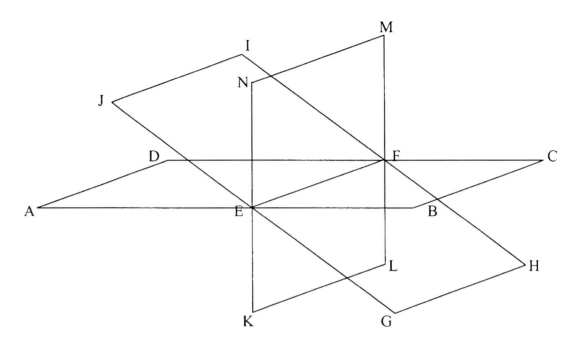

Use the above figure to determine the following questions:

6. <u>two</u> parallel lines

    a. $\overline{BC}$ and $\overline{GJ}$
    b. $\overline{KN}$ and $\overline{LM}$
    c. $\overline{HI}$ and $\overline{EF}$
    d. $\overline{JI}$ and $\overline{IH}$

7. <u>two</u> perpendicular lines

    a. $\overline{BC}$ and $\overline{GJ}$
    b. $\overline{KN}$ and $\overline{LM}$
    c. $\overline{HI}$ and $\overline{EF}$
    d. $\overline{JI}$ and $\overline{GH}$

8. <u>two</u> skew lines

    a. $\overline{BC}$ and $\overline{GJ}$
    b. $\overline{KN}$ and $\overline{LM}$
    c. $\overline{HI}$ and $\overline{EF}$
    d. $\overline{NM}$ and $\overline{KL}$

Content Cluster – STATISTICS, DATA ANALYSIS AND PROBABILITY
(Data Displays)

Objective: Students will know various forms of display for data sets, including a stem-and leaf plot or box-and-whisker plot; use them to display a single set of data or compare two sets of data.

Parent Tip: Stem-and-Leaf plots are means of organizing data. The leaf represents the last digit of the numbers and will <u>only</u> be a single digit. The stem represents <u>all</u> the rest of the digits in the number (when the leaves fall off, the stem remains). The stem-and-leaf plot must have a **key** telling you the value of one piece of data.

Examples: Set of Data – 10, 11, 11, 12, 19, 20, 22, 31, 33, 33

$$
\begin{array}{r|l}
\text{Stem} \rightarrow \quad 3 & 1 \ 3 \ 3 \\
2 & 0 \ 2 \qquad \leftarrow \text{Leaves} \\
1 & 0 \ 1 \ 1 \ 2 \ 9
\end{array}
$$

$$\text{key} \rightarrow \quad 2 \mid 0 \text{ means } 20$$

Mean = 20.2   **Median** = 19.5   **Range** = 33 – 10 = 23

Set of Data – 12.1, 12.1, 12.3, 12.4, 13.2, 13.4, 13.4

$$
\begin{array}{r|l}
13 & 2 \ 4 \ 4 \\
12 & 1 \ 1 \ 3 \ 4
\end{array}
$$

$$12 \mid 1 \text{ means } 12.1$$

Mean = 12.7   **Median** = 12.4   **Range** = 13.4 – 12.1 = 1.3

Use the stem-and-leaf plot for problems 1-6:

$$
\begin{array}{r|l}
4 & 6 \\
3 & 3 \ 5 \\
2 & 0 \ 0 \ 1
\end{array}
$$

$$2 \mid 0 \text{ means } 20$$

1. The stems are:

   a. 4, 6
   b. 3, 3, 5
   c. 2, 0, 0, 1
   d. 2, 3, 4

2. The leaves are:

   a. 2, 3, 4
   b. 2, 0, 0, 1
   c. 0, 0, 1, 3, 5, 6
   d. 2, 0, 0, 1, 3, 3, 4, 5, 6

3. The value of $3 \mid 3$ is:

   a. 33
   b. 3.3
   c. 0.33
   d. 330

4. What is the range?

   a. 20
   b. 26
   c. 33
   d. 35

5. What is the median?

   a. 21
   b. 26
   c. 27
   d. 33

6. What is the mean?

   a. 29.2
   b. 30.1
   c. 33.1
   d. 33.2

Use the stem-and-leaf plot for problems 7-12:

```
42 | 3
41 | 5  8
40 | 6  7
           40 | 6 means 40.6
```

7. The stems are:

   a. 3, 5, 8
   b. 6, 7, 8
   c. 40, 41, 42
   d. 43, 45, 46

8. The leaves are:

   a. 42, 3, 41
   b. 40, 41, 42
   c. 3, 5, 6, 7, 8
   d. 40, 46, 47

9. The value of 41 | 5 is:

   a. 41.5
   b. 4.15
   c. 0.415
   d. 415

10. What is the range?

   a. 0.3
   b. 1.7
   c. 1.6
   d. 2.0

11. What is the median?

   a. 42.3
   b. 41.5
   c. 41.8
   d. 40.7

12. What is the mean?

   a. 413.8
   b. 68.96
   c. 43.38
   d. 41.38

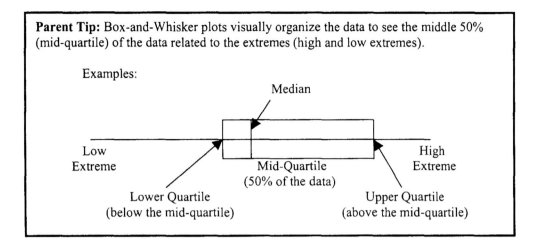

Parent Tip: Box-and-Whisker plots visually organize the data to see the middle 50% (mid-quartile) of the data related to the extremes (high and low extremes).

Examples:

Median

Low Extreme

Mid-Quartile (50% of the data)

High Extreme

Lower Quartile (below the mid-quartile)

Upper Quartile (above the mid-quartile)

Use the box-and-whisker plot for problems 13-16:

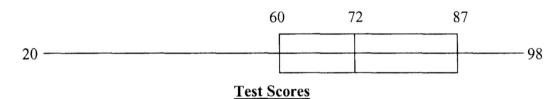

60   72   87

20 ———————————————— 98

Test Scores

13. What are the extremes of the data?

    a. 20 and 72
    b. 20 and 98
    c. 60 and 87
    d. 60 and 98

14. A score of 50 is located in the:

    a. lower quartile.
    b. mid-quartile.
    c. upper quartile.
    d. none of the above

15. A score of 90 is located in the:

    a. lower quartile.
    b. mid-quartile.
    c. upper quartile.
    d. none of the above

16. 50% of the students had scores between:

    a. 20 and 60
    b. 60 and 72
    c. 60 and 87
    d. 87 and 98

17. Which box-and-whisker plot shows the best test results?

    a.

    b.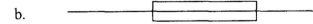

    c.

    d.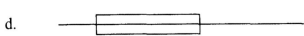

Content Cluster – STATISTICS, DATA ANALYSIS AND PROBABILITY
(Scatter Plot)

Objective: Students will represent two numerical variables on a scatter plot and informally describe how the data points are distributed and whether there is an apparent relationship between the two variables.

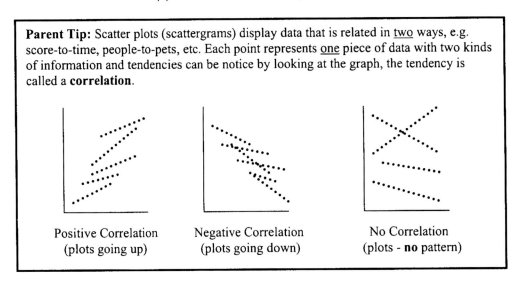

Parent Tip: Scatter plots (scattergrams) display data that is related in <u>two</u> ways, e.g. score-to-time, people-to-pets, etc. Each point represents <u>one</u> piece of data with two kinds of information and tendencies can be notice by looking at the graph, the tendency is called a **correlation**.

Positive Correlation
(plots going up)

Negative Correlation
(plots going down)

No Correlation
(plots - **no** pattern)

Use the scatter gram to answer questions 1-2:

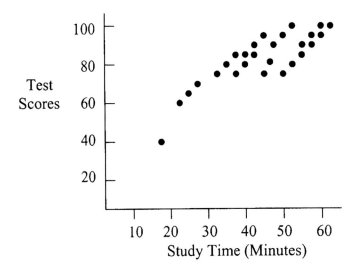

1. What type of correlation does the graph have?

    a. positive correlation
    b. negative correlation
    c. no correlation
    d. points

2. How many students took the test?

    a. 23
    b. 25
    c. 27
    d. not enough information

Use the set of data to answer questions 3-4:

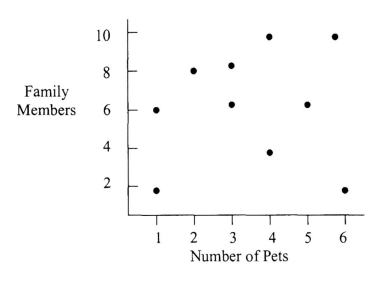

Survey of Families with Pets

3. What type of correlation does the graph have?

    a. positive correlation
    b. negative correlation
    c. no correlation
    d. points

4. How many families were surveyed?

    a. 8
    b. 10
    c. 12
    d. not enough information

5. Which scatter plot shows the correlation between children of age 0-5 years and their weight?

    a.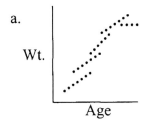

    b.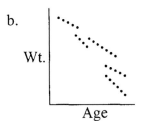

    c.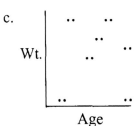

    d.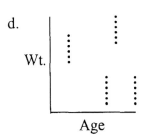

Content Cluster – STATISTICS, DATA ANALYSIS AND PROBABILITY
(Quartiles)

Objective: Students will understand the meaning of and be able to compute the minimum, the lower quartile, the median, the upper quartile and the maximum.

Parent Tip: The concepts in this cluster are based on the understanding of the vocabulary. Once this is known, the cluster is easy.

Definitions:
        Minimum – the smallest piece of data
        Maximum – the largest piece of data
        Median – the middle of the data
        Lower Quartile – the middle of the lower half of the data (minimum to median)
        Upper Quartile – the middle of the upper half of the data (median to maximum)

(This information is used to make box-and whisker plots.)

Example: **1, 1, 2, 3, 4, 4, 5, 6, 7, 7, 9, 10, 11, 11, 12**

Find the: 1) **Minimum** = 1
           2) **Maximum** = 12
           3) **Median** = 6 (there are 7 pieces of data above and below 6)
           4) **Lower Quartile** = 3 (there are 3 pieces of data above and below 3)
           5) **Upper Quartile** = 3 (there are 3 pieces of data above and below 10)

If there is an even amount of data, take the average of the 2 middle data and this will give the median of the set of data (the median is a location (**middle**) in the data, sometimes the location **isn't** in the data)

Use the set of data to answer questions 1-5:

60, 73, 74, 75, 75, 80, 81, 83, 88, 90, 95, 95, 98

1. Find the minimum.

    a. 90
    b. 98
    c. 60
    d. 80

2. Find the maximum.

    a. 90
    b. 98
    c. 60
    d. 80

3. Find the median.

    a. 80
    b. 81
    c. 83
    d. 88

4. Find the lower quartile.

    a. 73.5
    b. 74
    c. 75
    d. 74.5

5. Find the upper quartile.

    a. 91.5
    b. 92.5
    c. 93.5
    d. 94.5

Use the set of data to answer questions 6-10:

201, 202, 204, 210, 220, 225, 233, 240

6. Find the minimum.

    a. 201
    b. 204
    c. 220
    d. 240

7. Find the maximum.

    a. 201
    b. 204
    c. 220
    d. 240

8. Find the median.

    a. 210
    b. 220
    c. 215
    d. 225

9. Find the lower quartile.

    a. 201
    b. 202
    c. 203
    d. 204

10. Find the upper quartile.

    a. 225
    b. 229
    c. 233
    d. 240

Content Cluster – MATHEMATICAL REASONING
(Evaluating Information)

Objective: Students will analyze problems by identifying relationships, discriminating relevant from irrelevant information, identifying missing information, sequencing and prioritizing information, and observing patterns.

> **Parent Tips:** Read the problem more than once before starting it. Know what you are trying to find. See if there is enough information (missing), too much information (irrelevant), which order the information should be done (sequencing), or many times there is a pattern in the information that will help you solve it.

Read each problem and evaluate the information

1. Becky lives 3 miles from the store. She bought one gallon of milk for $3.15, a loaf of bread for $1.59 and a bottle of ketchup for $1.69. She was gone for 20 minutes. How much money did she spend at the store?

    a. irrelevant information
    b. missing information
    c. ready to solve

2. George brought 3 times as many newspapers to the school paper drive than Bill. Bill brought 15 more papers than Sue did. How many newspapers were brought to the paper drive?

    a. irrelevant information
    b. missing information
    c. ready to solve

3. Samantha and Sarah are sisters. Samantha is 2 years older than Sarah and has 3 goldfish. If each girl receives $5 allowance each week, how long will it take for the girls together to have $50?

    a. irrelevant information
    b. missing information
    c. ready to solve

4. Jamie lost 8 pounds the first month of her diet, 12 pounds the second month and 7 pounds the third month. How many pounds did she lose totally?

    a. irrelevant information
    b. missing information
    c. ready to solve

5. A train leaves the station at 8:00 AM going to Chicago. In Salt Lake City, 20 passengers get on and in Omaha 10 passengers get off. How many days did it take to get from Los Angeles to Chicago?

    a. irrelevant information
    b. missing information
    c. ready to solve

Read each problem and find the best approach to solve

6. At the clearance sale, Julie bought three dresses. One cost $24.95, another cost $39.95 and the last one cost $29.95. She gave the cashier a hundred dollar bill, how much change did she receive?

    a. sequencing information
    b. observe patterns
    c. ready to solve

7. John has $1,000 worth of Internet stock. He receives 10% interest every year on his stock. If he takes the interest out every year, how long would it take for him to get $400 from his interest?

    a. sequencing information
    b. observe patterns
    c. ready to solve

8. Jeremy's truck can hold 6 cases of product. He makes 3 trips to the market than makes 5 more trips with a trailer that can hold 2 cases of product. After the 8 trips, how many cases of product were delivered?

    a. sequencing information
    b. observe patterns
    c. ready to solve

9. When Courtney walks up the 15 steps to the room, she go up three and down one for more exercise. How many steps will she take to get to the top?

      a. sequencing information
      b. observe patterns
      c. ready to solve

10. A Mercedes Benz cost $63,955 and a Honda cost $17,645. How much more does the Mercedes cost than the Honda?

      a. sequencing information
      b. observe patterns
      c. ready to solve

Content Cluster – MATHEMATICAL REASONING (Simpler Parts)

Objective: Students will determine when and how to break a problem into simpler parts.

Parent Tips: Many times a problem needs to be broken down into smaller parts and solved <u>one</u> part at a time then put the parts together to answer the original problem.

Read each problem. Break into parts or ready to solve?

1. Jim is a delivery truck driver. Daily he drives 327 miles on his delivery route and 10 miles each way to work and back. How many miles does he drive in a 6-day workweek?

   a. break into parts
   b. ready to solve

2. Denise drove 4,238 miles on her National Parks vacation. Her car averaged 24 miles per gallon and she spent $259 for gas. How much did she pay per gallon for gas?

   a. break into parts
   b. ready to solve

3. It cost $1.25 to ride the city bus. At the end of the day, Stephanie deposited the cash box with $268.75 in it. How many passengers rode the bus?

   a. break into parts
   b. ready to solve

4. One high school 6-team football league decided to increase each team roster by 5 players. The rosters were at 40 players for each team, how many players are now on the roster?

   a. break into parts
   b. ready to solve

5. Steak is on sale for $1.99 per pound. How much does a 4.5-pound steak cost?

        a. break into parts
        b. ready to solve

6. A store bought 10 cases of eggs for $178.80. Each case has 12 dozen eggs. How much does a dozen eggs cost?

        a. break into parts
        b. ready to solve

Content Cluster – MATHEMATICAL REASONING
(Diagrams, Models, etc)

Objective: Students will use a variety of methods such as words, numbers, symbols, charts, graphs, tables, diagrams and models to explain mathematical reasoning.

> **Parent Tips:** Many times it is a good idea to put down the information visually using pictures, graphs, charts, diagrams, models, etc. Once you see what the problem "looks like", the reasoning skills needed to solve it becomes obvious – "A picture is worth a thousand words".

Which method would be best used to visualize the problem?

1. Marta took 3 short garden hoses and put them together to make a larger hose. The lengths of the hoses were 3 yards 1 foot, 5 yards, and 8 yards 1 foot. How long will the new hose be?

    a. table
    b. graph
    c. diagram
    d. model

2. With the first 5 books purchased, the store gives 1 book free. With the second 5 books purchased, you get 2 books free, the third 5 books purchased, get 3 books free and so on in the same pattern?

    a. table
    b. graph
    c. diagram
    d. model

3. It takes one machine 15 minutes to make a "What's-it-Called" and another machine 30 minutes to make it. If the 15 minute-machine was started 1 hour after the 30 minute-machine, how long will it take to make 8 "What's-it-Called"?

    a. table
    b. graph
    c. diagram
    d. model

4. Find the volume of a cylinder with a height of 5 inches and a diameter of 2 inches with a cone on top of it with the same diameter and a height of 3 inches?

      a.   table
      b.   graph
      c.   diagram
      d.   model

5. Brett makes $10.00 per hour plus 10% commission on every item he sells. How much must he have in average sales to make $2500 per month?

      a.   table
      b.   graph
      c.   diagram
      d.   model

6. Sally has a rectangular garden 12 feet by 9 feet. How many 3 feet by 3 feet smaller plots can be made within the garden?

      a.   table
      b.   graph
      c.   diagram
      d.   model

Content Cluster – MATHEMATICAL REASONING (Approximation)

Objective: Students will indicate the relative advantages of exact and approximate solutions to problems and give answers to a specified degree of accuracy.

> **Parent Tips:** When working on a problem or taking a multiple choice test an approximation of the answer can be useful in eliminating possible answers and increasing the possibility of being correct. Apply the rounding rules when using approximation.

Which would be the best approximation for each problem?

1. The cost of 4 items are $3.98, $2.19, $4.95 and $9.98. What is the total cost of all 4 items?

     a. $18.00
     b. $21.00
     c. $23.00
     d. $25.00

2. Ben has 11 sets of baseball cards. Each set has 28 cards in them. How many cards does he have in all?

     a.   150 cards
     b.   200 cards
     c.   250 cards
     d.   300 cards

3. Find the volume of a cylinder with a height of 8 inches and a base diameter of 2 inches.

     a.   16 cubic inches
     b.   18 cubic inches
     c.   24 cubic inches
     d.   32 cubic inches

4. The hotel bill came to $245. If it costs $49 per night to stay, how many nights did the family stay?

     a.   4 nights
     b.   5 nights
     c.   6 nights
     d.   7 nights

5. Joan is a bike rider. She rode 13.5 miles on Monday, 20.75 miles on Wednesday, and 25.25 miles on Friday. How many miles did she ride?

     a.   45 miles
     b.   55 miles
     c.   58 miles
     d.   60 miles

6. The bookstore sold 8,572 books last month and 10,585 books this month. How many total books were sold?

     a.   20,000 books
     b.   18,000 books
     c.   15,000 books
     d.   12,000 books

7. During the testing week at school the students took 5 tests. One 15 minute-test, a 30 minute-test, a 45 minute-test, an hour-test, and another 45 minute-test. How many hours were they tested?

     a.   1 hour
     b.   2 hours
     c.   3 hours
     d.   4 hours

8. Shirts are priced at $14.89 each, what will the price of 31 shirts be?

     a. $400
     b. $450
     c. $500
     d. $1,000

Content Cluster – MATHEMATICAL REASONING (Inductive/Deductive)

Objective: Students will make and test conjectures using both inductive and deductive reasoning.

Parent Tips: The definitions in this concept are very important and have to be thoroughly understood.

      Conjecture – to come to a conclusion based incomplete or inconclusive evidence

      Inductive Reasoning – to come to conclusions based on accepted principles

      Deductive Reasoning – to come to conclusions from knows facts

---

Inductive Reasoning

Is the statement true _always, sometimes, or never_?

1. A square is a rectangle.

    a. always
    b. sometimes
    c. never

2. An equilateral triangle is congruent to a right triangle.

    a. always
    b. sometimes
    c. never

3. A square has the same area and perimeter.

    a. always
    b. sometimes
    c. never

4. All circles are similar.

    a. always
    b. sometimes
    c. never

5. The probability of an event is greater than 1.

    a. always
    b. sometimes
    c. never

6. The product of two integers is greater than either integer.

    a. always
    b. sometimes
    c. never

7. A cylinder and a cone with the same base area and height have the same volume.

    a. always
    b. sometimes
    c. never

8. Two consecutive numbers are relatively prime.

    a. always
    b. sometimes
    c. never

9. The difference of two negative numbers is negative.

    a. always
    b. sometimes
    c. never

10. A scatter plot shows the relationship between two conditions of the data.

    a. always
    b. sometimes
    c. never

Deductive Reasoning

<u>Which is the best conclusion?</u>

11. All quadrilaterals have 4 sides. A rectangle has 4 sides. All squares are rectangles.

    a.   all rectangles are squares
    b.   all squares are quadrilaterals
    c.   all quadrilaterals are squares
    d.   all quadrilaterals are rectangles

12. The pattern is defined as x^2, what is the 10th number in this pattern?

    a.   20
    b.   30
    c.   50
    d.   100

13. Good readers are good students. Good students are good writers. Pete is a good writer.

    a.   all students are good readers
    b.   all students are good writers
    c.   Pete is a good reader
    d.   Pete is good in math

14. The diagonals in a polygon can be found by the formula $\dfrac{(n-3)n}{2}$, n = the number of sides in the polygon. How many diagonals are there in a nonagon?

       a.   18 diagonals
       b.   21 diagonals
       c.   24 diagonals
       d.   27 diagonals

15. On the number line, point A is greater than point B, point C is less than point B and point D is greater than point A.

       a.   point C has the least value
       b.   point A is less than point C
       c.   point B has the greatest value
       d.   point C is between points B and A

Content Cluster – MATHEMATICAL REASONING (Reasonable Answer)

Objective: Students will evaluate the reasonableness of the solution in context of the original problem.

Parent Tips: Once a problem is solved, check to make sure the answer makes sense based on the information in the problem.

Is the answer reasonable, unreasonable (too small) or unreasonable (too large)?

1. Jennifer is a waitress. Sunday through Wednesday she served 75 customers each day. On Friday she served 95 customers. How many customers did she serve?

   Answer → 200 customers

   a. reasonable
   b. unreasonable (too small)
   c. unreasonable (too large)

2. Tom and Jerry went on a camping trip. They stayed at campsites that cost $35 per day. The trip was for 1 week. How much did the campsites cost?

   Answer → $3500

   a. reasonable
   b. unreasonable (too small)
   c. unreasonable (too large)

3. A car is traveling at an average of 60 mph. How long will it take the car to travel 600 miles?

   Answer → 10 hours

   a. reasonable
   b. unreasonable (too small)
   c. unreasonable (too large)

4. A 50 foot by 100 foot field has fence post every 10 feet around the perimeter. How many post are there around the field?

   Answer → 30 posts

   a. reasonable
   b. unreasonable (too small)
   c. unreasonable (too large)

5. How many inches are there in 100 yards?

    Answer → 36 inches

    a. reasonable
    b. unreasonable (too small)
    c. unreasonable (too large)

6. Sue can types 435 words in 5 minutes. How many words can she type in 1 minute?

    Answer → 87 words

    a. reasonable
    b. unreasonable (too small)
    c. unreasonable (too large)

7. Each school bus carries 45 students. How many buses are needed for 300 students?

    Answer → $6\frac{1}{2}$ buses

    a. reasonable
    b. unreasonable (too small)
    c. unreasonable (too large)

8. The bank pays 7% interest per year on savings account, how much interest would you receive after 1 year on $10,000 account?

    Answer → $7000

    a. reasonable
    b. unreasonable (too small)
    c. unreasonable (too large)

MATH ANSWER KEY

Number Sense

Scientific
Notation
1. a
2. d
3. b
4. b
5. c
6. c
7. d
8. a
9. c
10. d
11. a
12. a
13. b
14. b
15. c
16. d
17. c
18. a
19. d
20. c

Computation
Skills
1. b
2. d
3. d
4. c
5. a
6. a
7. c
8. c
9. b
10. d
11. c
12. b
13. a
14. b
15. a
16. b
17. b
18. a
19. b
20. c
21. d
22. a

23. a
24. c
25. a
26. d
27. d
28. b
29. c
30. c
31. d
32. b
33. a
34. a
35. d
36. c
37. b
38. c
39. d
40. b
41. b
42. a
43. c
44. c
45. d
46. a
47. b
48. a
49. b
50. b
51. c
52. c
53. d
54. b
55. a
56. c
57. b
58. b
59. d
60. b
61. c
62. c
63. b
64. a
65. a
66. a
67. c
68. b
69. c
70. d

71. a
72. b
73. d
74. d
75. b
76. b
77. c
78. b
79. b
80. d

Whole
Numbers/Powers
1. c
2. b
3. c
4. a
5. d
6. c

Convert Fractions
1. b
2. a
3. c
4. a
5. d
6. d
7. b
8. a
9. c
10. d
11. d
12. b
13. a
14. c
15. c

Decimals/Percents
1. a
2. a
3. d
4. c
5. b
6. d
7. a
8. c
9. d
10. b

11. d
12. c
13. d
14. c
15. a

Rational/Irrational
1. a
2. a
3. b
4. a
5. a
6. b
7. a
8. a
9. b

Terminating/
Repeating
1. b
2. a
3. b
4. b
5. a
6. a
7. b
8. b
9. a

Decimal/Fractions
1. b
2. d
3. b
4. c
5. a
6. b
7. b
8. a
9. c
10. b
11. d
12. d

Percent Increase/ Decrease
1. b
2. d
3. b
4. a
5. b
6. a
7. c
8. c
9. b

Discounts/ Markups
1. c
2. b
3. b
4. d
5. a
6. d
7. b
8. b
9. c
10. b

Negative Exponents
1. b
2. c
3. d
4. c
5. a
6. b
7. d
8. d
9. a

Squares and Roots
1. b
2. d
3. a
4. b
5. c
6. d
7. a
8. c
9. b

Estimate Square Roots
1. a
2. d
3. b
4. c
5. c
6. d
7. a
8. b

Absolute Value
1. b
2. a
3. b
4. b
5. a
6. a
7. b
8. a
9. a

Algebra and Functions
Verbal to Problem
1. c
2. a
3. d
4. b
5. a
6. a
7. c
8. d
9. a
10. a
11. b
12. b
13. a
14. c
15. d
16. a
17. b
18. c
19. a
20. c
21. b
22. d
23. a
24. d
25. a

Evaluate Expressions
1. d
2. b
3. b
4. a
5. c
6. d
7. a
8. c
9. c
10. a
11. c
12. b

Simplify Expressions
1. b
2. c
3. a
4. c
5. c
6. b
7. d
8. c

Algebraic Terminology
1. b
2. c
3. a
4. d
5. c
6. d
7. b
8. d
9. a

Graphical Interpretation
1. c
2. b
3. a
4. c
5. b
6. c
7. b
8. c

Positive/Negative Powers
1. c
2. a
3. a
4. c
5. b
6. d
7. c
8. c
9. a
10. d
11. b
12. c

Monomials
1. d
2. a
3. b
4. a
5. c
6. a
7. d
8. b
9. b

(y=2n)
1. a
2. a
3. b
4. b
5. a
6. b
7. a
8. b
9. b
10. a
11. b
12. d

Slope
1. c
2. d
3. d
4. a
5. d
6. b
7. a
8. d
9. d
10. a

Two-Step Equations

1. c
2. b
3. b
4. d
5. d
6. a
7. c
8. a
9. c

Multi-Step Problems

1. a
2. d
3. b
4. d
5. c
6. a

Measurement and Geometry

Compare Measurements

1. a
2. c
3. d
4. a
5. a
6. b
7. c
8. d
9. a
10. d
11. b
12. b
13. a
14. d
15. c

Perimeter, Area, Volume

1. c
2. b
3. a
4. c
5. c
6. d
7. a
8. c

9. c
10. b
11. c
12. c
13. a
14. a
15. c
16. a

Complex Figures

1. c
2. b
3. a
4. c
5. d
6. a

Scale Factor

1. b
2. a
3. d
4. b
5. b
6. d

Change Measurement

1. b
2. d
3. a
4. c
5. a
6. b
7. c
8. b
9. a
10. d
11. c
12. a
13. d
14. a
15. c
16. b
17. c
18. c

Coordinate Graph

1. c
2. a
3. b
4. c

5. d
6. a
7. a
8. b
9. a
10. b

Pythagorean Theorem

1. c
2. b
3. c
4. a
5. d
6. a
7. c
8. b
9. d

Congruency

1. b
2. c
3. a
4. c
5. b
6. d
7. c
8. a
9. d

3-D Figures

1. b
2. c
3. a
4. d
5. c
6. b
7. c
8. a

Statistics, Data Analysis and Probability

Data Displays

1. d
2. c
3. a
4. b
5. c
6. a
7. c

8. c
9. a
10. b
11. b
12. d
13. b
14. a
15. c
16. c
17. a

Scatter Plot

1. a
2. c
3. c
4. b
5. a

Quartiles

1. c
2. b
3. b
4. d
5. b
6. a
7. d
8. c
9. c
10. b

Mathematical Reasoning

Evaluating Information

1. a
2. b
3. a
4. c
5. b
6. a
7. b
8. a
9. b
10. c

Simpler Parts

1. a
2. a
3. b
4. a
5. b
6. a

Diagrams,
Models

1. c
2. a
3. b
4. d
5. a
6. c

Approximation

1. b
2. d
3. c
4. b
5. d
6. a
7. c
8. b

Inductive/
Deductive

1. a
2. c
3. b
4. a
5. c
6. b
7. c
8. a
9. b
10. a
11. b
12. d
13. c
14. d
15. a

Reasonable
Answer

1. b
2. c
3. a
4. a
5. b
6. a
7. b
8. c

SOCIAL SCIENCE

World History and Geography: Medieval and Modern Times

Content Cluster: THE CAUSES AND EFFECTS OF THE EXPANSION AND SUBSEQUENT DECLINE OF THE ROMAN EMPIRE.

Objective: To evaluate knowledge of: (1) the strengths and contributions of Rome; (2) the impact of Rome's geographic borders; and (3) the development of the Byzantine Empire and the later growing schism between Roman Catholicism and Eastern Orthodoxy.

> **Parent tip:** In assisting students in the understanding of social science, it is sometimes helpful to examine themes both throughout history and within cultures. For example, economic factors like trade have brought new products and culture into different areas. Geographic features have protected civilizations from conquest, and have allowed people to develop societies independent from outside contact.

Directions: Choose the best answer for the following questions.

1. In the ancient Roman empire, barbarians were considered to be

   a. primitive people.
   b. people living along the Mediterranean Sea.
   c. people living along Rome's borders.
   d. people living in Egypt.

2. People living along Rome's eastern and central borders had

   a. blue eyes and reddish hair.
   b. quick tempers.
   c. strong bodies.
   d. a and c

3. The first emperor of Rome was

   a. Caesar Augustus.
   b. Julius Caesar.
   c. Constantine.
   d. Diocletian.

4. By C.E.117, Rome had reached its greatest size. It extended from Scotland in the north, to Africa in the south, and from the Atlantic Ocean in the west, to _____ in the east.

   a. India
   b. China
   c. Israel
   d. Syria
   e. Egypt

5. Provinces were areas

   a. outside the jurisdiction of Rome.
   b. inside Italy.
   c. outside Italy and ruled by Rome.
   d. none of the above

6. Provinces were valuable to Rome because

   a. they provided buffer zones protecting the Empire.
   b. they provided food and natural resources.
   c. they provided manpower for the legions and taxes for the government.
   d. all of the above
   e. b and c only

7. Rome supported the provinces by

   a. building roads and aqueducts.
   b. providing protection in case of attack.
   c. insisting that people living along the borders live like Romans.
   d. a and c only
   e. a and b only

8. The final collapse of the Western Roman Empire occurred in

   a. 44 B.C. E.
   b. C. E. 410
   c. C. E. 476
   d. C. E. 732

9. Roman emperors increased the size of the Roman Empire by

   a. conquering new territory.
   b. enlisting barbarians into the Roman legions.
   c. building new cities.
   d. none of the above

10. Rome's contributions to architecture include

    a. Doric, Ionic, and Corinthian columns.
    b. the arch, the dome, and the column.
    c. the post and lintel.
    d. the pulley.

11. Latin as a language enabled which religion to spread throughout the Empire?

    a. Islam
    b. Judaism
    c. Christianity
    d. Zoroastrianism

12. Which emperor declared that upon his death, the Roman Empire should be split in two?

    a. Diocletian
    b. Julius Caesar
    c. Augustus
    d. Theodosius

13. Internal problems that helped create Rome's downfall were

    a. barbarian invasions.
    b. ambitious generals and civil wars.
    c. economic problems.
    d. the Greeks.
    e. b and c

14. Which of the following was **not** a reason Rome declined?

    a. The Byzantines became too strong.
    b. The Roman army was too expensive.
    c. The barbarians invaded the Roman Empire.
    d. Roman armies fought among themselves.
    e. Rome became too large to govern.

Content Cluster: THE ORIGIN, GROWTH, AND EXPANSION OF ISLAM IN THE MIDDLE EAST AND THE GROWTH OF CITIES AND TRADE ROUTES IN ASIA, AFRICA, AND EUROPE.

Objective: To assess knowledge of: (1) the geographical factors of the Arabian peninsula; (2) the origin, development, and spread of Islam and the Arabic language; (3) the growth of cities along trade routes and the exchange of products and ideas; (4) the contributions of Muslim scholars.

> **Parent tip:** The achievements Muslim scholars made to later civilizations were significant. Likewise, the Islam religion has become an important influence in today's world. Discuss these ideas with your student in tandem with the beginnings of both the Islam religion and the Muslim culture; specifically, the importance of adaptations made by these early peoples to the environment of the Arabian Peninsula and adjacent areas.

Directions: Choose the best answer for the following questions.

1. Areas in deserts which get water from wells or underground springs are

   a. rivers.
   b. streams.
   c. meadows.
   d. oases.

2. Nomads wandered across the Arabian peninsula looking for

   a. the suburbs.
   b. food and water.
   c. grazing areas for their animals.
   d. a and b
   e. b and c

3. Irrigation systems in the Middle East were both underground and along streams using

   a. water wheels.
   b. hydroelectric plants.
   c. reservoirs.
   d. dams.

4. The word Quraysh means

    a. a food made of cheese and other ingredients
    b. a holy book.
    c. the name of a tribe settling in Mecca
    d. the name of a ruler in Petra

5. Which of the following is <u>not</u> one of the Five Pillars of Islam?

    a. the Hajj
    b. the Sunna
    c. the fast during Ramadan
    d. prayer

6. The written record of Allah's words revealed to Muhammad is

    a. the Sunna
    b. the jihad
    c. the Torah
    d. the Qur'an

7. Muhammad, while in a desert cave, saw a vision of _____ who commanded him to recite.

    a. Gabriel
    b. Moses
    c. David
    d. Jesus
    e. Abraham

8. A belief that there is only one God is

    a. animism
    b. monotheism
    c. polytheism
    d. humanism

9. The collection of the words and deeds of Muhammad written down after several generations is called the

    a. Qur'an
    b. Quraysh
    c. Old Testament
    d. Sunna

10. A Muslim house of worship is a

   a. temple.
   b. church.
   c. synagogue.
   d. mosque.

11. Which of the following bodies of water does **not** surround the Arabian Peninsula?

   a. The Red Sea
   b. The Mediterranean Sea
   c. The Persian Gulf
   d. The Dead Sea
   e. The Arabian Sea

12. According to Islamic teachings, the Ka'bah was

   a. built by Abraham and Jacob on the site of the city of Mecca.
   b. completed by Ishmael after his father died.
   c. the god who protected the idols.
   d. built by Abraham and Ishmael to remind everyone of Abraham's belief in God.

13. The Umayyad Empire collapsed because

   a. the exchange of trade goods had diminished.
   b. taxes were reduced because many non-Muslims had converted to Islam.
   c. the Abbasids thought that the Umayyads had lost sight of Muhammad's ideals.
   d. a and b
   e. b and c

14. Bagdad became the center and capital city of the Abassid Empire. The area was an excellent location for a city because

   a. it was situated between the Tigris and Euphrates Rivers.
   b. it was situated along major East – West trade routes.
   c. it was closer than Damascus to the area of the birth of Islam.
   d. a and b
   e. a and c

Content Cluster: CHINA'S GEOGRAPHY AND ITS IMPACT ON POLITICAL, ECONOMIC, AND RELIGIOUS DEVELOPMENT; EMPHASIZING INVENTIONS AND DISCOVERIES.

Objective: To evaluate student knowledge of: (1) the reunification of China and the spread of Buddhism; (2) the technological, agricultural, and economic advancements during the Tang and Sung dynasties; (3) the influences of Buddhism and Confucianism on Chinese thought; (4) the growth of a money economy within China and interactions with other civilizations; and (5) the influence of China's inventions and discoveries throughout the world.

Parent tip: The Chinese civilization has had significant impact on world societies. Despite being isolated for much of its productive history, China's inventions and discoveries made their way to the Middle East and Europe, even though this movement took centuries in most cases. Discoveries such as gunpowder, and inventions such as the magnetic compass and the printing press paved the way for the spread of the Renaissance in Europe and exploration throughout the world. Parallel timelines are a great method of comparing Chinese discoveries with corresponding ideas in other areas of the world.

Directions: Choose the best answer for the following questions.

1. Which of these ideas was **not** part of Buddhism?

    a. suffering is a part of life
    b. life is a cycle of death and rebirth
    c. meditation
    d. proper conduct

2. Physical barriers on the _____ protected and isolated China.

    a. west, north, and south
    b. east, southwest, and west
    c. east, north, and south
    d. west, east, and south

3. Emperor Wen encouraged the practice of

    a. Daoism.
    b. Confucianism.
    c. Islam.
    d. Buddhism.

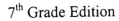

4. Geography created regions within China that made it difficult to unify. An example of this was the _____.

    a. Great Wall
    b. Grand Canal
    c. Taklimakan Desert
    d. Qin Ling Mountains

5. In the Sui and early Tang dynasties, aristocrats

    a. held most jobs in the government.
    b. could study for the civil service exams.
    c. neither a nor b
    d. both a and b

6. Respect for elders, proper conduct, and scholarship are key elements of

    a. Confucianism.
    b. Buddhism.
    c. Daoism.
    d. none of the above

7. What is the name for a system in which people are chosen for employment and are able to move up within an organization?

    a. aristocracy
    b. democracy
    c. oligarchy
    d. meritocracy

8. Tang and Sung painters portrayed human figures as small. This appears to show that

    a. they could not draw human figures.
    b. they liked to paint landscapes better than humans.
    c. humans are not as important as the beauty of nature.
    d. humans have a very small part in the natural world.
    e. c and d

9. The aristocrats lost power in the civil service system because

    a. their population decreased.
    b. their qualifications were not as demanding as earlier.
    c. the system was opened to members of other social classes.
    d. the system was replaced by the emperor.

10. During the 700's improved transportation enabled messengers and other government officials to travel more efficiently throughout China. These improvements included

    a. canals and waterways
    b. freeways
    c. roads
    d. a and b
    e. a and c

11. In addition to improved transportation, a new quick growing _____ helped support an increasing population.

    a. wheat
    b. barley
    c. corn
    d. rice
    e. none of the above

12. Extra products, which are not needed, may be sold or traded. These can be called

    _____.

    a. goods
    b. surplus
    c. taxes
    d. treaties

13. A money economy is

    a. based on a barter system.
    b. an economy in which cash is commonly used in exchange for goods.
    c. used to judge the value of goods.
    d. none of the above

14. Which of these inventions was not Chinese?

    a. the idea of algebra
    b. printing
    c. fishing reel
    d. paper currency

15. Movable type enabled Chinese scholars to quickly copy

    a. Greek and Roman classics.
    b. African legends.
    c. Confucian classics.
    d. none of the above

Content Cluster: CONTRIBUTIONS OF SUB-SAHARAN AFRICAN CIVILIZATIONS DURING THE MEDIEVAL PERIOD

Objective: To assess the student's knowledge of: (1) principle climate regions in the Sub-Sahara and their impact on the growth of civilizations; (2) the development of Ghana, Mali, and Songhai as empires (3) the importance of trans-Saharan trade especially in gold and salt; (4) the beliefs, education, and written language of the Muslims in the growth and spread of African culture.

Parent tip: The information about African societies, which has been published recently, is valuable to everyone. Check out a bookstore or the Internet to locate a book of African tales (many of which were told orally for generations), or one about accomplishments of these civilizations. Many were far more advanced than their contemporaries in Europe during the Middle Ages.

Directions: Choose the best answer for the following questions.

1. Most people in West Africa lived

    a. along rivers.
    b. in large cities.
    c. in small villages.
    d. in the deserts.

2. The person who helped people communicate with the Gods was called

    a. a chief.
    b. a diviner.
    c. an ancestor.
    d. a griot.

3. The person who told stories was usually

    a. a chief.
    b. a diviner.
    c. an ancestor.
    d. a griot.

4. Who was the great emperor who traveled to Mecca with "80 to 100 camels, each loaded with 100 pounds of gold dust"?

   a. Sumangruru
   b. Mansa Musa
   c. Ibn Battuta
   d. Sunni Ali
   e. none of the above

5. The empire of _____ fell in the Battle of Kirina in 1235.

   a. Ghana
   b. Mali
   c. Songhai
   d. Zimbabwe

6. The Nok people moved to areas along the Niger River to find

   a. gold.
   b. silver.
   c. iron.
   d. farmland.

7. West African terrain consisted primarily of

   a. grasslands and forests.
   b. scattered vegetation.
   c. desert.
   d. tundra.

8. Many West African societies practiced matrilineal succession. This means that

   a. descent is traced through the males of society.
   b. in order to succeed you must be female.
   c. in order to succeed you must be male.
   d. descent is traced through the females of society.

9. Which of the following factors was **not** critical in establishing Ghana as an important trading area?

   a. Ghana was along the coastline.
   b. Ghana was at the center of a major trade route.
   c. Salt and gold were close to equal in value.
   d. Salt was a necessity in the diet of West Africans.

10. Berber tribesmen who lived along "the shore of the desert", an area known as the _____ carried goods across the Sahara.

   a. savanna
   b. rain forest
   c. river basin
   d. sahel

11. The new empire of Mali was governed by _____. He had defeated Sumanguru, the last of the Soninke kings.

   a. Sunni Ali
   b. Askia Muhammad
   c. Sundiata
   d. Mansa Musa

12. Which ideas did Muslim traders bring to West African societies?

   a. a system of numbers
   b. a system of writing
   c. the Islamic religion
   d. all of the above
   e. a and c only

13. Koumbi, Ghana's capital and trading center was divided into two sections. One was for the Muslims and the trade area; the other was for the local people and the_____.

   a. Berber chief
   b. Swahili army
   c. Merchants
   d. Soninke king

14. The rulers of Mali re-established the trans-Saharan trade routes and also used the _____ River to transport gold from the newly discovered gold fields.

   a. Niger
   b. Nile
   c. Congo
   d. none of the above

15. Which of these Sub-Saharan civilizations does **not** have a present-day country with the same name?

    a. Ghana
    b. Mali
    c. Songhai
    d. a and b
    e. a and c

16. Askia Muhammad was best known as

    a. a non-Muslim who attempted to drive out of Songhai all those who were believers in Islam.
    b. the military leader who defeated Mansa Musa.
    c. the ruler who unified the empire of Songhai by expanding its borders and establishing learning and trade centers.
    d. none of the above

17. Which of the following puts the three empires of West Africa in the correct order, from earliest to latest?

    a. Songhai, Mali, Ghana
    b. Ghana, Mali, Timbuktu
    c. Mali, Ghana, Morocco
    d. Ghana, Mali, Songhai

18. The Almoravids, by conquering Koumbi for a brief period,

    a. took over the trade routes.
    b. contributed to the fall of Ghana.
    c. helped the spread of Arabic writing.
    d. rebuilt the city.

19. Kinship or family relationships formed

    a. the new trade routes in West Africa.
    b. new dances in the communities.
    c. the political and religious structure in West Africa.
    d. new ties with the Berber peoples.

Content Cluster: THE DEVELOPMENT OF JAPAN DURING THE MEDIEVAL PERIOD

Objective: To evaluate students' knowledge of: (1) Japan's location and corresponding influence of neighboring countries on its development; (2) Japan's societal values, social customs, and traditions as practiced through time; (3) the significance of religion and cultural achievements in art and literature.

> **Parent tip:** The physical forces that are inherently a part of the Pacific Rim played a critical role in the shaping of Japanese civilization, as did the cultural influences of China and Korea. Although Japan's culture grew in relative isolation, many of Japan's traditions have lasted for centuries. Help your student understand Japan's role in the global world in which we live.

Directions: Choose the best answer for the following questions.

1. Zen Buddhism

   a. took the place of Shinto as Japan's major religion.
   b. stressed respect for elders and proper conduct.
   c. taught that spiritual discipline and enlightenment was not of value.
   d. appealed to many samurai were illiterate and welcomed a move away from book learning.

2. Which of the following was **not** a part of the Tokugawa shogunate?

   a. The shogunate lasted for more that 250 years.
   b. The shogunate banned Christianity.
   c. The shogunate opened new trade routes to Europe.
   d. The shogunate established a line of succession.

3. Which of the following was true about Japan's early cultures?

   a. The Jomon were most likely trading people from western Asia.
   b. A more permanent society, the Yayoi were able to grow rice in water.
   c. The "tomb culture" filled burial sites with metal tools.
   d. None of the above

4. Japanese mythology holds that the beginning of the world

   a. occurred when Izanagi withdrew his jeweled spear from the ocean forming islands.
   b. occurred as a tremendous series of volcanoes pushed land out of the Pacific Ocean.
   c. started as the Storm God created a typhoon with his sword.
   d. started when the Storm God's descendents defeated the forces of Evil.

5. Courtiers were

   a. merchants who were employed by the emperor.
   b. members of the powerful Fujiwara clan.
   c. monks who lived in monestaries and wrote manuscripts.
   d. members of the (imperial) court and who took part in its social life.

6. The sea was important to Japan's development because

   a. it was a major resource.
   b. it surrounded the Japanese islands, thereby isolating them.
   c. it supported Japan's vast naval power.
   d. all of the above
   e. a and b only

7. Physical qualities of Japanese women which were admired included

   a. blackened teeth.
   b. hair as long as or equal to her height.
   c. shaved eyebrows.
   d. all of the above
   e. b and c only

8. Which of the following was **not** part of or a result of the Taika Reforms?

   a. Public works projects were established.
   b. All farmland became property of the emperor.
   c. The leaders of clans were chosen to supervise plots of farmland.
   d. The lives of the peasants were not changed.

9. Kanji was

   a. a writing system which originated and was simplified in Japan.
   b. a system of writing which used phonetic symbols of single syllables.
   c. a writing system which was based on Chinese characters.
   d. a writing system which was based on Egyptian hieroglyphics.

10. Which of the following is true about the Japanese feudal system?

    a. Shoguns served the daimyo warriors in protecting the estates.
    b. Samurai warriors won pieces of land for protecting the estates.
    c. Daimyos were clan leaders.
    d. Daimyos pledged allegiance to samurai warriors.

11. In the Japanese social system,

    a. the peasants were the lowest in the hierarchy.
    b. the artisans were the highest of the classes.
    c. the merchants were the lowest in the hierarchy before the growth of a money economy.
    d. the samurai relaxed in the court of the emperors.

12. New cultural forms grew in the 1600's as members of the lower part of the social strata utilized new leisure time. Some of these forms were

    a. haiku poetry.
    b. short stories.
    c. Kabuki theater.
    d. all of the above
    e. a and c only

13. Shinto, Japan's main religion holds that

    a. everything in the natural world is filled with spirits.
    b. everything is in harmony with nature.
    c. life is a cycle of death and rebirth.
    d. proper conduct and respect for elders is the basis of belief.

14. A military life known as _____, the way of the warrior, was characterized by early weapon training and commitment to a strict lifestyle.

    a. Shogun
    b. Samurai
    c. Daimyo
    d. Bushido

Content Cluster: DEVELOPMENT AND CHANGES DURING THE MIDDLE AGES IN EUROPE.

Objective: To assess knowledge of geographic, economic, political, religious, and social structures of Medieval Europe

> **Parent tip:** In the wake of the chaos that once was Rome, grew a society that initially was anything but civilized, but one that eventually evolved into one of democratic thought and constitutional practice. One cannot discount the role of the Church and the monarchies in this development. As you discuss these institutions, a main concept is the interrelationship among the social, religious, and political structures as the change from a medieval society to one that is enlightened occurs. A second idea on which to focus involves the growth of small towns into larger cities and the corresponding trade based on the demand for eastern goods introduced to Europe by the Crusaders and travelers.

Directions: Choose the best answer for the following questions.

1. The stated purpose of the Crusades was to

   a. encourage the exchange of Muslim ideas with those of Europe.
   b. establish strong central governments in the Middle East.
   c. insure the safe travel of Christians who wished to travel to the Holy Land.
   d. to open trade routes between Europe and the Middle East.

2. As a result of the Crusades,

   a. the Church gained power in both Europe and the Middle East.
   b. ideas and products were introduced to Europe.
   c. new religions were brought to Europe.
   d. permanent settlements were established in the Middle East.

3. Castles became obsolete in part because

   a. a new breed of horse from Asia appeared in Europe.
   b. people in Europe lived in peace.
   c. gunpowder was introduced in Europe.
   d. they had all been destroyed in battle.

4. A monastery during the Middle Ages

    a. served as a outpost of learning.
    b. had beautiful flying buttresses.
    c. was self-sufficient.
    d. all of the above
    e. a and c only

5. During the early Middle Ages which of the following is most accurate?

    a. Schools were started in the manors.
    b. Invasions of Europe came from both the sea and over land.
    c. Zen Buddhism was introduced into Spain.
    d. Charles Martel brought the Islamic religion with him from Spain to France.

6. Which of the following was **not** one of Charlemagne's accomplishments?

    a. learned to read and write
    b. defeated both the Slavs and the Lombards
    c. was crowned Holy Roman Emperor
    d. reduced Church corruption

7. Improved technology helped increase farming production. Which of the following were ways in which this was done?

    a. Horseshoes allowed some farmers to use horses instead of oxen.
    b. Avocados and oranges supplied variety to the people's diet.
    c. Metal-tipped plows allowed farmers to reach deeper into the soil.
    d. a and b
    e. a and c

8. A guild was

    a. a group of craftspeople possessing the same skill.
    b. a tournament event.
    c. a guarded entrance to a castle.
    d. a series of tasks to be performed by knights.

9. If any group lived a comfortable life during the Middle Ages, they were

    a. the lords of the feudal manors.
    b. the serfs.
    c. the clergy.
    d. knights mounted on horseback.

10. The construction of a cathedral was a colossal decision and an even greater task. It was the life's work of most of the townspeople. The building of a cathedral was so important

    a. because it was a monument to the glory of God and the power of the church.
    b. because it would not be completed for generations.
    c. in that it would provide many jobs for the townspeople.
    d. because it would raise taxes.

11. Under feudalism, people received protection from large landowners in return for

    a. military service for about forty days each year.
    b. working on the lord's land.
    c. performing necessary tasks such as repairing roads or bridges, working in the mill, or gathering wood.
    d. all of the above
    e. a and b only

12. Vassals were

    a. merchants who served the king.
    b. enemies who had been captured in battle.
    c. landowners who had given title of their estates to the feudal lord.
    d. both a and c

13. Henry IV had difficulties with Pope Gregory VII because

    a. he took exception to the Pope's document that stated that the Church should have the power to appoint Church officials.
    b. he was threatened with excommunication.
    c. the Pope's army was too strong.
    d. a and b only
    e. b and c only

14. As a result of the struggles between kings and popes over authority, the Concordat of Worms was signed in 1122. This document gave the

    a. pope the right to appoint church leaders.
    b. kings the right to appoint church leaders.
    c. nobles the right to approve the church's recommendations.
    d. none of the above

15. Which of the following was **not** a result of the Crusades?

    a. The Jewish population in both Europe and the Middle East was attacked by Christians.
    b. The Holy Land was returned to the Christians.
    c. Christians were allowed to keep some areas north of Jaffa.
    d. Christians burned and looted Constantinople.

16. Which quality was least important in feudalism?

    a. courtesy
    b. loyalty
    c. bravery
    d. obedience
    e. individualism

17. The Magna Carta was one of the most important documents that came out of the Medieval period because

    a. it made official the idea that ordinary people had rights.
    b. it set the basis for the idea of "due process of law".
    c. it stated that the king was subject to the law of the land.
    d. all of the above

18. The code of honor among knights during the Middle Ages, chivalry taught that knights should

    a. be fair, courteous, and exhibit honor and loyalty.
    b. be strong in all their affairs.
    c. show poor sportsmanship in tournaments.
    d. chase the servants around the castle.

19. The vassal swears allegiance to his lord in a ceremony

    a. which is not open to the public.
    b. called dubbing.
    c. which was a code of honor.
    d. which was known as act of homage.

20. Because monks and priests were among the only members of society who could read and write, the Church was a leader in the

    a. organization of governments, and the preparation of documents.
    b. preservation of manuscripts.
    c. education of society and the eventual founding of universities.
    d. all of the above

21. Jews were often _____ by Christians.

    a. accepted
    b. ignored
    c. persecuted
    d. befriended
    e. c and d

22. In Spain, during the Umayyad period, Christians and Jews were

    a. not allowed freedom to worship.
    b. fighting against the Muslims.
    c. fighting between themselves.
    d. working with Muslims to translate books into Latin.

23. When the city of Toledo fell to the Christians in 1085, it marked the beginning of the end of Muslim control of Spain. This period was called

    a. the Crusades.
    b. the Reconquest.
    c. the Renaissance.
    d. the Enlightenment.

24. Charles Martel was one of the great leaders during the early Middle Ages, even though he was never a king. He held the position of

    a. Lord of the Manor.
    b. Monk.
    c. Mayor of the Palace.
    d. King's Advisor.

25. Cordoba had more than 70 libraries, 200,000 people, beautiful palaces and mosques. It was capital of the Ummayad Islamic Empire in

    a. France.
    b. Syria.
    c. Italy.
    d. Spain.

Content Cluster: THE MESOAMERICAN AND ANDEAN CIVILIZATIONS.

Objective: To evaluate the knowledge of: (1) the geographical features which influence the Mayan, Inca, and Aztec economies and cultural organization; (2) the social class structure within each society; (3) the effect of the Spanish conquerors on the people and their societies;(4) the lasting contributions of the Mayan, Inca, and Aztec civilizations.

> **Parent tip:** One of the more interesting ideas to appear as your student examines this section is that some of the innovations and achievements which occurred in the Middle East or Asia also arose in Mesoamerica at the same with no apparent contact between the groups. The technique of drawing parallel timelines between these cultures is a way to visually compare inventions and discoveries.

Directions: Choose the best answer for the following questions.

1. Early people in the Americas

    a. migrated to the new land by means of a land bridge through Greenland and Canada.
    b. may have traveled to North and South America by boat.
    c. migrated to the new land by means of a land bridge across the Bering Sea between Alaska and Siberia.
    d. a and b only
    e. b and c only

2. Clues from homes of both hunter-gatherers and sedentary village dwellers were hard for archaeologists to determine because

    a. little remained of their structures.
    b. neither group used shelter.
    c. hunter-gatherers did not stay in one place very long.
    d. both used stone foundations.

3. The Olmec civilization which existed from about 1200 until 400 B.C.E.

    a. lived along the coastlines and were able to live from fishing.
    b. invented an elaborate irrigation system.
    c. had spiritual, military, and government officials called priest-kings.
    d. was destroyed by a series of earthquakes.

4. Mayan civilization was based on agriculture. Which statement is true regarding their methods of farming?

  a. In the lowlands they grew crops raised on terraces.
  b. In the high ground they burned jungles.
  c. They dug moats and canals to bring water to arid places.
  d. They used a pump system to raise water to the highland areas.

5. The Maya thought that priests could interpret the will of the gods by studying the two Mayan calendars. With the help of math also, the priests could

  a. help the people determine if a certain day was better than another to plant crops.
  b. figure out which gods controlled which days.
  c. determine the mood of the gods.
  d. all of the above

6. Which of the following was **not** a Mayan achievement?

  a. number system
  b. codices
  c. hieroglyphs
  d. gold and jade jewelry

7. Aztec farming methods made use of floating gardens called

  a. chinampas.
  b. calpullis.
  c. terraces.
  d. moats.

8. The Aztec settled in a swampy island in Lake Texcoco because

  a. they were forced there by enemies.
  b. it was an area free from insects.
  c. other tribes had chosen the most fertile land in the area.
  d. they saw an eagle on the island.

9. Aztecs learned to be skillful warriors by

  a. fighting against neighboring tribes.
  b. fighting for neighboring tribes.
  c. fighting in a civil war.
  d. fighting for Portugal.

10. As part of Inca religion,

    a. rulers were mummified in part to prevent spirits from harming the people.
    b. rulers brought mummies out for special ceremonies.
    c. the Inca built temples for the sun god, Inti.
    d. all of the above
    e. a and b only

11. A vertical economy was a system

    a. of growing crops where each crop or food is above the other.
    b. in which each crop is worth more than the previous one.
    c. of arranging crops or food according to altitude.
    d. none of the above

12. Inca administrators had the unique job of

    a. sending scouts to potential areas that were going to be conquered to assess the fertility of the soil.
    b. attempting to persuade enemy tribes to join the Inca.
    c. both a and b
    d. neither a nor b

13. Commoners who were not needed in farming activities were

    a. allowed to relax in the house of the ruler.
    b. put to work on huge public projects.
    c. sacrificed.
    d. elevated to the post of government official.

14. The Inca differed from the Maya and the Aztec in that they

    a. traveled long distances to trade.
    b. lived along the Amazon River.
    c. had no written language.
    d. were non-violent.

15. Which of the following is **not** a related element of Aztec sacrifice?

    a. The Aztec wanted to frighten their enemies.
    b. They believed that if one were sacrificed, he would become divine.
    c. They wanted to fight against other tribes to capture prisoners to sacrifice.
    d. They loved to watch people die.

16. Similar problems facing both the Aztec and the Inca created weakened empires by the time the Spanish arrived in the New World. Which were problems that affected the empires?

    a. Civil war caused both empires to lose strength.
    b. Disease killed many Aztec and Inca soldiers.
    c. Religious differences caused misunderstandings.
    d. a and c only
    e. a, b, and c

17. A calpulli is

    a. a narrow strip of farming land built in a swamp.
    b. a currency used in trade.
    c. a settlement of Aztec people of different social classes.
    d. a hieroglyph written on a large stone.

18. The Mayan number system was based on 20 with

    a. values from one to 100 in increments of 20.
    b. place values up to the 1000's place.
    c. symbols drawn as pictures.
    d. certain symbols such as dashes indicating various numerical values.

19. Sedentary groups of people would

    a. need water and a food source like fish or corn to remain in one location.
    b. migrate following herds of animals.
    c. usually build homes they could take with them.
    d. vanish as the animals they followed became extinct.

20. Technique used by the Inca to raise crops on mountain slopes was known as

    a. irrigation.
    b. terrace farming.
    c. floating gardens.
    d. crop rotation.

Content Cluster: THE RENAISSANCE: ORIGINS, GROWTH AND SPREAD OF IDEAS AND ACHIEVEMENTS.

Objectives: To evaluate knowledge of: (1) the renewal of interest in Greek and Roman classics; (2) the importance of Italian city-states in the establishment and growth of Renaissance ideas; (3) the inventions, discoveries, and spread of ideas throughout Europe; and (4) the achievements of people like Leonardo da Vinci, Michelangelo, and William Shakespeare.

Parent tip: Familiarize yourself with the fascinating ideas and achievements of the Renaissance. They did not merely occur all over Europe simultaneously, but progressed with the work of many groups of people over hundreds of years. Help your student understand the role of each of these groups, whether they are artists, merchants, monarchs, patrons, or scientists and how their cooperation assisted in making this one of the most exciting periods in man's development.

Directions: Choose the best answer for the following questions.

1. This person was famous for writing *Utopia*?

    a. Shakespeare
    b. Voltaire
    c. Sir Thomas More
    d. da Vinci

2. Major ideas of the Renaissance included

    a. realism.
    b. humanism.
    c. individualism.
    d. all of the above
    e. a and c only

3. Italy became a center of the early Renaissance due in part to

    a. its location.
    b. its ancient history.
    c. its strong central government.
    d. a and c only
    e. b and c only

4. Even though the Church remained powerful during the Renaissance it was not as strong as it had been the past because

    a. the Church had lost much of its wealth.
    b. Protestantism spread throughout Europe.
    c. people were more interested in the arts than religion.
    d. European states became more powerful.
    e. b and d only

5. What motivated explorers to try to find the shortest way to the East?

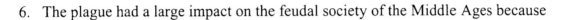

    a. slaves
    b. weapons
    c. spices
    d. freedom

6. The plague had a large impact on the feudal society of the Middle Ages because

    a. it created a shortage of workers.
    b. peasants demanded higher payment for work.
    c. peasants moved to town to find new jobs.
    d. all of the above
    e. b and c only

7. Which of the following was **not** a reason that warfare changed.

    a. the development of longbows
    b. the development of better armor
    c. the development of harquebusses
    d. a and b
    e. a and c

8. Persons who concerned themselves with the Greek and Roman classics and saw the importance of public service were

    a. humanists.
    b. individualists.
    c. realists.
    d. linguists.
    e. anarchists.

9. Heretics were people who were not accepted by the Church because

    a. they wore long hair.
    b. they had different views from the Church.
    c. they had ticks in their hair.
    d. they believed in the Pope.

10. A major difference between the Renaissance in northern Europe and that in Italy was that_____.

    a. art and learning were more important in Italy
    b. wealthy families in northern Europe formed democracies
    c. nobles in Italy rejected the Renaissance
    d. monarchs and nobles in northern Europe and ruling families in Italy were the major patrons of Renaissance artists

11. Renaissance artists depicted people as they really appeared. They also used the idea of_____.

    a. religious subjects
    b. linear perspective
    c. mixing oil with paint
    d. b and c
    e. a and b

12. Mercenaries were paid by many city-states to

    a. guard shipments of gold bullion.
    b. travel with merchants.
    c. fight as soldiers for the control of global trade markets.
    d. research the most profitable trade routes.

13. Leonardo da Vinci was famous for his painting, science discoveries, and accomplishments in many other areas. Among his creative ideas were the drawings for_____.

    a. planes, trains, and automobiles
    b. a horseless carriage
    c. a parachute
    d. a and b
    e. b and c

14. Patrons were extremely important during the Renaissance because they

    a. provided money for artists and writers to complete their works.
    b. allowed shopkeepers to keep their stores open longer.
    c. helped merchants exchange their trade items.
    d. could worship everyday.

15. During the Renaissance, Jews, were still prohibited from owning land, and they were first restricted to certain neighborhoods called

    a. developments
    b. villages.
    c. towns.
    d. ghettos.

16. Michelangelo, a foremost artist during the Renaissance studied the human anatomy so that he could

    a. become a doctor.
    b. draw and sculpt the human figure realistically
    c. collect human organs.
    d. become a professor.

17. William Shakespeare, an actor, a poet, and possibly the world's greatest playwright, revealed strengths and weaknesses of humans through his characters. Most of Shakespeare's plays may be classified into three types

    a. comedies, histories, and documentaries.
    b. documentaries, portraits, and biographies.
    c. biographies, comedies, and tragedies.
    d. comedies, histories, and tragedies.

18. Johannes Gutenberg helped spread Renaissance ideas with the European invention of the_____.

    a. sure-footed pack mule
    b. telegraph
    c. printing press
    d. movable type printing press

19. Which of the following is a true statement about the Italian Renaissance?

    a. Life on earth is not important; only life after death is critical.
    b. Women are equal to men all aspects of society.
    c. All people should have an equal in say in how their government runs.
    d. Wealthy persons in society should use some money for public good.

20. Life for the common person during the Renaissance

    a. improved due to the new products introduced to Europe through trade.
    b. improved through education.
    c. remained much like it had been during the Middle Ages.
    d. provided time for them to be creative.

21. Black Death (the plague) moved across Europe rapidly from 1347 to 1353. It was carried by fleas on rats living on trade ships traveling between

    a. Africa and Europe.
    b. Asia and Europe.
    c. North America and Europe.
    d. Africa and North America.

22. The Medici family of Florence controlled

    a. a system of international banks in Europe.
    b. European trade with China.
    c. leather making in Florence.
    d. building trade in Venice.

23. Miguel de Cervantes was famous for writing

    a. The Prince.
    b. Hamlet.
    c. Don Quixote.
    d. Book of the Family.

24. "If any woman becomes so proficient as to be able to write down her thoughts, let her do so and not despise the honor…" These words were spoken by

    a. Hildegard
    b. Louise Labe
    c. Shakespeare
    d. Sir Thomas More

Content Cluster: THE REFORMATION AND ITS HISTORICAL DEVELOPMENT

Objective: To assess the student's knowledge of: (1) causes of the decline of the Catholic church; (2) the major ideas of people such as; Martin Luther and John Calvin and their impact on Protestantism; (3) the split between Protestantism and the Catholic church; (4) the work of Muslims and Jews in Spain and the movement toward intolerance.

> **Parent tip:** This is an appropriate time to discuss intolerant behavior as exhibited in Europe through the Spanish Inquisition and, later, the persecution of many religious groups both in Europe and America. Courageous individuals such as Martin Luther and John Wycliff led the way as they challenged the Catholic Church.

Directions: Choose the best answer for the following questions.

1. The authority of the Catholic church decreased largely as a result of

   a. poor leadership.
   b. the view among English, Germans and the Italian city-states that France exerted greater authority over the Church than others.
   c. the struggle between France and the Church, which ultimately resulted in the Catholic church having two popes at the same, time (the Great Schism).
   d. a and b
   e. b and c

2. Councils were

   a. members of cities who met to decide where new buildings were to be built.
   b. groups of people elected to make decisions on city matters.
   c. groups of Church leaders, who made decisions on church business.
   d. groups of Church leaders who made laws.

3. What do the following people have in common? John Calvin, Martin Luther, John Wycliff, and Ulrich Zwingli.

   a. They all wanted to increase taxes for the Church.
   b. They were all monks.
   c. They all wanted to be leaders in the Catholic Church.
   d. They all protested against Church practices like excessive taxes and indulgences.

4. That God has determined all things ahead of time as well as salvation is known as

   a. primogeniture.
   b. preservation.
   c. prehistoric.
   d. predestination.

5. Martin Luther believed that

   a. priests should not have any special powers because they were priests.
   b. the Bible was the authority for Christians, not Church laws.
   c. the policy of racial equality should be made law.
   d. a and c
   e. a and b

6. An agreement called the_____ allowed each prince in his area in Germany to decide whether Protestantism or Catholicism would be followed.

   a. Peace of Augsburg
   b. Council of Trent
   c. Concordat of Worms
   d. Magna Carta

7. The end of a "Golden Age" of achievements in Spain occurred as

   a. Muslims and Jews both made pilgrimages to the Holy Land.
   b. the Inquisition was revived to help establish the new Spanish state.
   c. Ferdinand expelled all Jews from Spain.
   d. a and b only
   e. a and c only

8. The Counter Reformation was

   a. an attempt to remodel a counter.
   b. an attempt to reform the new Protestant religions.
   c. an attempt to restore basic Catholic beliefs and get rid of corruption.
   d. none of the above

9. The Calvinists, followers of John Calvin, believed that

   a. one should lead a simple life and be devoted to God.
   b. nothing should interfere with individual experience with God.
   c. a code of behavior was not important.
   d. all of the above
   e. a and b only

10. Justification by faith, a key idea of Martin Luther, held that

   a. individuals could achieve forgiveness on their own.
   b. the Church could grant forgiveness of sins.
   c. a person could achieve forgiveness if he accepted God.
   d. everyone should worship together to gain forgiveness.

11. The *Ninety-Five Theses* of Martin Luther stated

   a. his reasons for wanting to become a priest in the Catholic church.
   b. his opposition to the discovery of the New World.
   c. that the earth revolved around the sun.
   d. his objections to the corruption within the Catholic church and the practice of selling indulgences.

12. By the mid-16th century, areas of Europe that were primarily Catholic included Spain, France, and Italy, while the countries of _____ were largely Lutheran.

   a. Germany, Prussia, and Norway
   b. Germany, Switzerland, and Denmark
   c. Germany, Hungary, and Poland
   d. Germany, England, and Sweden

13. In addition to the main goals of the Council of Trent, the Catholic church promoted special religious orders to help spread the ideas of the Church. An example of one of these was the

   a. Calvinists
   b. Jesuits
   c. Puritans
   d. Christians

14. A different reform movement occurred in England as Henry VIII demanded that the Church grant him a divorce. He prohibited all foreign authorities which resulted in

   a. a return to basic beliefs.
   b. the publication of the pamphlet, *"Against the Robbing and Murdering Hordes of Peasants"*.
   c. the invention of the movable type printing press.
   d. Parliament's passing the "Act of Supremacy" which established the Church of England.

15. One of John Wycliff's defiant acts was to translate the Bible from Latin into English. This was a problem because

   a. the power of the clergy was threatened because they could read Latin.
   b. more Bibles were printed in English than Latin.
   c. the monks could only copy manuscripts in Latin.
   d. none of the above

Content Cluster: THE SCIENTIFIC REVOLUTION AND ITS IMPACT ON RELIGIOUS, POLITICAL, AND SOCIAL THOUGHT

Objective: To evaluate student's knowledge of: (1) the basis of scientific thought and information gained through exploration and trade; (2) the significance of new theories and inventions; and (3) scientific method and its influence on political and religious ideas of the time period.

> **Parent tip:** A correlation may be drawn between early religious ideas of the Reformation and those of the Scientific Revolution. Reformers sought to challenge Church beliefs, while scientists questioned classical ideas regarding the universe and other physical theories. It would be advantageous to learn the basic contributions of scientists like Newton, Galileo, Hooke, and Vesalius.

Directions: Choose the best answer for the following questions.

1. Galileo's ideas challenged beliefs of the Catholic church because

   a. the earth-centered universe was the accepted view.
   b. no one had ever proposed such a theory before.
   c. the sun-centered theory did not place the earth (humans) in the middle of God's plan.
   d. a and b
   e. a and c

2. Galileo made new discoveries through observation. Among them were the

   a. discovery of sunspots.
   b. discovery of blood circulation.
   c. theory of oval planet orbits.
   d. theory of relativity.

3. The influence of Muslim scholars was transported to Europe through trade and by encounters with the Crusaders. Which of the following were **not** Muslim advancements?

   a. astronomy and geometry
   b. medicine
   c. mathematics
   d. philosophy
   e. none of the above

4. Scientific method, a major idea from this period.

    a. Was a series of steps using observation and experimentation in research.
    b. Allowed Francis Bacon to win the Nobel prize for philosophy.
    c. Included a hypothesis which could be verified by testing.
    d. all of the above
    e. a and c only

5. Robert Hooke was famous for

    a. inventing a new telescope.
    b. dissection of human hanging victims.
    c. discovering forces which pull objects toward the center of the earth.
    d. inventing a new type of microscope which produced a clearer magnification.

6. Nicolaus Copernicus may be thought of as

    a. one of the first thinkers to understand the inhumane nature of the Inquisition.
    b. the scientist who discovered Jupiter's moons.
    c. one of the first scientists to use data obtained from accurate observation to refute accepted beliefs.
    d. a foremost leader of the Reformation.

7. Both scientists and Reformation leaders had the following in common

    a. they both believed that they had no choices in church matters.
    b. they both used scientific method in their research.
    c. they both questioned ideas which had existed for centuries.
    d. they valued Eastern religions instead of Catholicism.

8. Which of the following statements about Isaac Newton is **not** true?

    a. He had logical explanations regarding forces in the universe.
    b. He discovered that the force called gravity held the universe together.
    c. Newton was a mathematician.
    d. He published a book called, "Utopia".

9. Aside from its use, what was a revolutionary aspect of scientific method?

    a. It allowed the Church to continue its persecution of non-believers.
    b. The idea that people cannot learn by accepting truths.
    c. It was a challenge to ruling systems throughout Europe.
    d. It prevented meaningful discoveries.

10. One of Johannes Kepler's contributions to astronomy was that

    a. orbits of the planets were round.
    b. planets orbited around the earth.
    c. planets orbited around the sun at the same rate.
    d. orbits of the planets were oval.

11. Andreas Vesalius a Flemish scientist admitted he had dissected human bodies. This was a problem because

    a. no one had ever done this before.
    b. people thought he was crazy.
    c. dissection was prohibited by the major religions, Christianity, Islam, and Judaism.
    d. Vesalius could not find the bodies.

12. Edward Jenner, through a series of experiments, discovered

    a. a vaccine for small pox.
    b. a vaccine for cowpox.
    c. cowpox and small pox were related.
    d. both a and c

13. The Catholic Church admitted the error of condemning this scientist almost 300 years after the fact.

    a. Galileo
    b. Copernicus
    c. Francis Bacon
    d. Vesalius

14. What was the period of time during the 15th and 16th centuries characterized by new scientific ideas and the challenge of existing beliefs?

    a. The Renaissance
    b. The Reformation
    c. The Enlightenment
    d. The Scientific Revolution

Content Cluster: THE AGE OF EXPLORATION, THE ENLIGHTENMENT, AND THE AGE OF REASON

Objective: To assess the student's knowledge of the political and economic changes during the sixteenth, seventeenth, and eighteenth centuries.

Parent tip: This is a conglomeration of many elements, which influenced not only Europe, but Asia, Africa, and the newly discovered Americas. At the center of it all was trade. Help your student understand the concept of supply and demand as it applied to Europe. The values of reason, observation, and examination provided the basis for the Enlightenment.

Directions: Choose the best answer for the following questions.

1. Philosophes were

    a. a group of Greek philosophers.
    b. a collection of books written by European writers.
    c. the European thinkers and writers of the 1700s.
    d. the standards by which scientists were judged.

2. The Renaissance was an important period to Enlightenment thinkers because

    a. paintings were more realistic.
    b. the ancient Greek and Roman ideals were all that could be learned.
    c. humanists believed in the importance of the individual.
    d. humanists thinkers believed that if people could understand the world, they could improve it.
    e. both c and d

3. The Age of Enlightenment was a optimistic time for many people because

    a. they felt threatened by the change.
    b. they thought that through reason new ideas could help improve society.
    c. they felt that governments were able to meet the individuals' needs.
    d. they were comfortable with the new technology.

4. One of the major ideas of the Enlightenment was

    a. the application of principles of physics to biology.
    b. using the ideas of philosophy to improve scientific discoveries.
    c. applying economic principles from Asia to America.
    d. applying the principles of scientific reason to social and political problems.

5. John Locke wrote *Two Treatises of Government* in 1690. In it he argued that

    a. an agreement between people and their ruler called a contract was the basis of government.
    b. people had a right to overthrow the ruler if the contract was not followed.
    c. each person had the rights of life, liberty, and property protection.
    d. all of the above
    e. a and b only

6. Baron de Montesquieu argued that a king or queen's power should be limited. He thought that the best way to do this was to

    a. separate the government into legislative, executive, and judicial branches.
    b. make sure the army could control the monarch.
    c. elect the monarch.
    d. reason the monarch into protecting the rights of the people.

7. Jean-Jacques Rousseau believed

    a. that people should participate in his or her own government.
    b. that if a government did not serve the needs of its people, the contract could be cancelled.
    c. none of the above
    d. a and b

8. Benjamin Franklin and Thomas Jefferson studied the ideas of the philosophes and used their ideas ultimately to

    a. write the Constitution of the United States.
    b. declare independence from England.
    c. reject British rule.
    d. a and b only
    e. a and c only

9. Agricultural improvements such as the enclosure of farmland, crop rotation, and _____ helped boost production.

    a. the flying shuttle
    b. the spinning jenny
    c. the horse-drawn seed drill
    d. the turnip planter

10. New information from travelers such as Marco Polo and Ibn Battuta, improved maps and inventions that reached Europe and created

    a. interest in geography.
    b. desire for items such as silk, gold and spices.
    c. interest in exploration.
    d. a and b
    e. b and c

11. Among the people to profit from the expansion between Europe and the areas of Southeast Asia were merchants in the Italian city-states of

    a. Florence and Rome.
    b. Rome and Venice.
    c. Genoa and Venice.
    d. Paris and Genoa.

12. Portugal was one of the countries in Europe lacking exports to match the imports its people demanded. They sometimes owed money to other countries. Therefore, in order to maintain this "balance of trade" Portugal needed

    a. diamonds.
    b. spices.
    c. silk.
    d. gold.

13. Portugal attempted to break the monopoly of the Italian merchants by

    a. hiring north African traders instead.
    b. traveling to America.
    c. finding new sources of silk.
    d. finding a direct sea route to the East.
    e. c and d

14. Bullion is

    a. a soup made from lentils.
    b. gold or silver bars of a certain weight.
    c. a new type of ship.
    d. a splint used for bracing broken bones.

15. Deists were

    a. religious thinkers.
    b. peasants.
    c. believers in Tao.
    d. people against the Church.

16. Voltaire was known as one of the most important_____ of the Enlightenment.

    a. poets
    b. tyrannical kings
    c. priests
    d. writers

17. The *Encyclopedie*, written by Denis Diderot, is

    a. an early form of the dictionary.
    b. volumes of history books.
    c. a collection of writings by many authors.
    d. a collection of childrens' stories.
    e. an early form of encyclopedias.

18. Natural rights were rights guaranteed to all including

    a. life, liberty, and the pursuit of happiness.
    b. life, liberty, with no responsibilities.
    c. life, liberty, and right to own property.
    d. the right to petition.

19. The Industrial Revolution

    a. brought about new computer access.
    b. brought about change in the way goods were produced.
    c. provided a new opportunity for workers coming to the cities.
    d. b and c

SOCIAL SCIENCE ANSWER KEY

Rome
1. c
2. d
3. a

Islam
1. d
2. e
3. a
4. c
5. b
6. d
7. a
8. b
9. d
10. d
11. d
12. d
13. e
14. d

China
1. d
2. b
3. d
4. a
5. d
6. c
7. d
8. e
9. c
10. e
11. a

12. b
13. b
14. a
15. c

Africa
1. c
2. b
3. d
4. b
5. a
6. c
7. a
8. d
9. a
10. c
11. c
12. d
13. d
14. a
15. c
16. c
17. d
18. b
19. c

Japan
1. d
2. c
3. b
4. a
5. d
6. e
7. d
8. d
9. c
10. b
11. c
12. e
13. a
14. d

European Middle Ages
1. c

2. b
3. c
4. e
5. b
6. a
7. e
8. a
9. c
10. a
11. d
12. c
13. a
14. a
15. b
16. e
17. d
18. a
19. d
20. d
21. c
22. d
23. b
24. c
25. d

Meso-America
1. e
2. a
3. c
4. c
5. d
6. e
7. a
8. e
9. b
10. d
11. c
12. c
13. b
14. c
15. d
16. e

17. c
18. d
19. a
20. b

Renaissance
1. c
2. d
3. a
4. d
5. c
6. d
7. b
8. a
9. b
10. d
11. d
12. c
13. e
14. a
15. d
16. b
17. d
18. e
19. d
20. c
21. b
22. a
23. c
24. b

Reformation
1. e
2. c
3. d
4. d
5. a
6. a
7. c
8. c
9. e
10. c
11. d
12. a

13. b
14. d
15. a

Scientific Revolution
1. e
2. c
3. e
4. e
5. d
6. c
7. c
8. d
9. b
10. d
11. c
12. d
13. a
14. d

Enlightenment Exploration and Reason
1. c
2. e
3. b
4. d
5. d
6. a
7. b
8. e
9. c
10. e
11. c
12. d
13. d
14. b
15. a
16. d
17. c
18. c
19. d

SCIENCE

Content Cluster- LIFE SCIENCE (CELL BIOLOGY)

Objective: To learn some of the basic cell parts and their function. In addition, the student will learn the difference between animal and plant cells and the basic type of cell organization.

> **Parent Tip:** Cells are the basic building blocks of living things, just as bricks are the basic structural units of many buildings. Cells are found in a variety of shapes and sizes, but have many parts, whose functions are the same in all cells. Plants cells and animal cells do have some differences, but both divide through a process called mitosis to increase their numbers. Unicellular organisms are living things that exist as a single cell. Multicellular (many cells) organisms are more complex and can have groups of cells organized into tissues, organs, and systems.

1. The cell theory states which of the following?

   a. all organisms are composed of cells
   b. cells are the basic unit of structure and function in organisms
   c. all cells come from other cells
   d. all of the above

2. An exception to the cell theory is the _____.

   a. virus
   b. unicellular organism
   c. human
   d. multicellular organism

3. A cell's shape is related to its function. What is the shape of the skin cells whose function is protection?

   a. cube-like with cilia
   b. flat and in layers
   c. spherical and fluid-filled
   d. long columns in a single layer

4. Cells that do not have a nucleus are called _____.

   a. eukaryotic cells
   b. multicellular cells
   c. unicellular cells
   d. prokaryotic cells

5. Cells in a human have a nucleus and are called _____.

    a. prokaryotic cells
    b. colonial cells
    c. eukaryotic cells
    d. unicellular cells

6. Bacteria are examples of _____.

    a. prokaryotic cells
    b. eukaryotic cells
    c. nucleated cells
    d. multicellular cells

7. The tiny structures that perform functions within a cell are called _____.

    a. organelles
    b. organs
    c. tissues
    d. cytoplasm

8. The organelle that manufactures protein and is found in all organisms is called the

    a. nucleus.
    b. lysosome.
    c. vacuole.
    d. ribosome.

9. Plant cells are different from animal cells in that they have another layer that surrounds the outside of the cell called the _____.

    a. plasma membrane
    b. chloroplast
    c. cell wall
    d. nuclear membrane

10. The function of the mitochondria in a cell is to

    a. convert light to chemical energy for use in the cell.
    b. store food and water for the cells later use.
    c. make proteins.
    d. release energy from food.

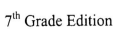

11. The cell wall found in plants is made of _____.

    a. protein
    b. lipid
    c. cellulose
    d. chitin

12. Organelles found only in animal cells that contain digestive enzymes used by the cell to breaks down large molecules or worn out cell parts are called _____.

    a. lysosomes
    b. ribosomes
    c. mitochondria
    d. chloroplasts

13. Which is not a function of the nucleus in a cell?

    a. to control cellular activities
    b. to carry and transfer genetic information
    c. to provide energy to the cell
    d. to provide instructions for the building of proteins

14. What is the function of the large central vacuole in a plant cell?

    a. to defend against infection
    b. to hold fluid under pressure, keeping the plant upright
    c. to make food for the plant to use
    d. to make more cells used in plant growth

15. Which structure in the cell contains the genetic material called DNA?

    a. mitochondria
    b. nucleus
    c. plasma membrane
    d. chloroplast

16. Photosynthesis is the process of making sugar (glucose) from light energy. In this process which of the following materials is released?

    a. carbon dioxide
    b. nitrogen
    c. oxygen
    d. sodium

17. The green pigment that is important for photosynthesis is called

    a.   xanthrophyll
    b.   carotene
    c.   hemoglobin
    d.   chlorophyll

18. The process of photosynthesis occurs in

    a.   aquatic animals.
    b.   plants and algae.
    c.   humans.
    d.   terrestrial animals.

19. What are the structures that carry the hereditary information (DNA) from one generation to the next?

    a.   nuclear pores
    b.   Golgi bodies
    c.   chromosomes
    d.   ribosomes

20. What is the process of cell division in most animal and plant cells?

    a.   photosynthesis
    b.   mitosis
    c.   lysis
    d.   combination

21. Cells divide for all the following reasons except:

    a.   to increase the size of the organism
    b.   to repair an injury
    c.   to replace worn out parts
    d.   to prevent the need for water

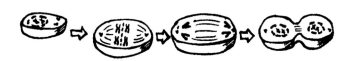

22. Which is the first phase of cell division?

    a.   prophase
    b.   metaphase
    c.   telophase
    d.   anaphase

23. What is the stage of the cell cycle in which the cell is not dividing but performing normal activity?

   a. prophase
   b. interphase
   c. metaphase
   d. cytokinesis

24. During mitosis, the chromosomes will line up on the equator of the cell before moving to the opposite sides. When they line up in this central position, this is called

   a. prophase
   b. anaphase
   c. telophase
   d. metaphase

25. When a cell divides by the process of mitosis, the resulting two cells have

   a. the same number of chromosomes, but different genetic material
   b. the same number of chromosomes and identical genetic material
   c. one half the number of chromosomes as the parent cell
   d. twice the number of chromosomes as the parent cell

26. What is the division of the cytoplasm after mitosis?

   a. meiosis
   b. cytokinesis
   c. anaphase
   d. fertilization

27. Multicellular organism have _____.

   a. organs
   b. tissues
   c. organ systems
   d. all of these

28. The function of the chloroplast, found only in a plant cell, is to:

   a. make proteins from other materials
   b. transform light energy to chemical energy
   c. move the cell into the sunlight
   d. package material received from the roots

29. An organism that exists as a single cell is called a:

    a.   multicellular organism
    b.   unicellular organism
    c.   recellular organism
    d.   dicellular organism

30. The structure common to both plants and animals that controls movement of materials into and out of the cell is called:

    a.   the nucleus
    b.   a chromosome
    c.   the cell wall
    d.   the plasma membrane

Content Cluster-LIFE SCIENCE (GENETICS)

Objective: To introduce the study of genetics, heredity, and cell reproduction. The student will learn the basic processes and the vocabulary needed to understand the subject.

Parental Tip: Heredity is the passing of traits or physical characteristics from parent to offspring. The study of heredity is called genetics. DNA is the genetic material of all living organisms. This material is found on small units called genes located on structures called chromosomes. These structures are located in the nucleus of the cell. Every physical characteristic is controlled by at least one pair of genes. Some genes are dominant and mask the effects of the other gene in the pair, the recessive gene. The genes in the cells called the genotype determine the appearance of the organism or phenotype. When only one parent produces an offspring, the process is called asexual reproduction. Sexual reproduction requires two parents and the creation of eggs and sperm. Each sperm or egg has one half the number of chromosomes that the other cells of an organism have.

---

1. What is the scientific study of heredity?

    a. evolution
    b. genetics
    c. botany
    d. zoology

2. Which of the following men is known as the "father of genetics?"

    a. Charles Darwin
    b. Louis Pasteur
    c. Gregor Mendel
    d. James Watson

3. The type of reproduction that requires only one parent is called?

    a. sexual
    b. regeneration
    c. asexual
    d. fusion

4. If a normal human body cell has 46 chromosomes how many chromosomes are in a human sex cell (egg or sperm)?

    a. 46
    b. 92
    c. 4
    d. 23

5. What is the cell that results from the fertilization of an egg by a sperm?

    a. zygote
    b. sex cell
    c. gamete
    d. body cell

6. What is the ability to replace lost body parts or the development of a new animal from parts of another animal?

    a. budding
    b. binary fission
    c. spore formation
    d. regeneration

7. What are the different forms of a particular gene that can be passed on to an offspring?

    a. alleles
    b. mutations
    c. zygotes
    d. chromosomes

8. What is the joining of two cells one from each parent to form an offspring?

    a. budding
    b. sexual reproduction
    c. regeneration
    d. all of these

9. Asexual reproduction includes:

    a. binary fission
    b. budding
    c. vege 'ative propagation
    d. all of these

10. A physical characteristic that an organism inherits from the parents is called

  a. a mutation
  b. a trait
  c. replication
  d. intelligence

11. Genes that are in an organism that prevent other genes from being expressed are called

  a. dominant genes
  b. recessive genes
  c. duplicate genes
  d. misgenes

12. The way an organism appears is called it's

  a. genotype
  b. phenotype
  c. homozygous appearance
  d. gene pool

13. What are the segments on a chromosome that control the appearance of a specific characteristic?

  a. carbohydrates
  b. proteins
  c. genes
  d. zygotes

14. If a plant producing red flowers is crossed with a plant with white flowers and all the offspring produce red flowers, then

  a. red flowers are recessive to white flowers
  b. white flowers are dominant to red flowers
  c. white flower are recessive to red flowers
  d. no conclusion can be made

15. Which of the following are not gametes?

  a. eggs
  b. sperm
  c. ovum
  d. zygotes

16. What is an organism that has two of the same alleles of a gene for a trait?

    a.   homozygous
    b.   heterozygous
    c.   a hybrid
    d.   clone

17. What is the formation of sex cells in living organism?

    a.   mitosis
    b.   binary fission
    c.   budding
    d.   meiosis

18. The X and Y chromosomes determine which of the following in animal offspring?

    a.   intelligence
    b.   height
    c.   athletic ability
    d.   sex (male or female)

19. Human females have

    a.   one X and one Y chromosome
    b.   two Y chromosomes
    c.   two X chromosomes
    d.   none of the above

20. What are the crosses involving the alleles of only one gene to determine the results in offspring?

    a.   monohybrid crosses
    b.   dihybrid crosses
    c.   polygenic crosses
    d.   monogenic crosses

21. What is the main function of the genes on chromosomes?

    a.   control the production of proteins
    b.   control the production of carbohydrates
    c.   control the production of lipids
    d.   control the production of brain cells

22. An allele that is determined to be dominant is represented by a

    a.   small-case letter
    b.   capital letter
    c.   italic letter
    d.   numeral

23. To have a recessive trait expressed in an individual, the organism must have

    a.   both recessive genes
    b.   one recessive gene
    c.   both parents expressing the trait
    d.   one parent expressing the trait

24. Which of the following is a homozygous dominant genotype?

    a.   Hh
    b.   hh
    c.   HH
    d.   all of these

25. An animal that has a Y chromosome is a

    a.   female
    b.   male
    c.   mutant
    d.   clone

26. If two heterozygous black cats (carrying the genes for black and white hair) produced four offspring, how many of them would you expect to have white hair?

    a.   4
    b.   3
    c.   2
    d.   1

27. If a homozygous black cat is cross with a homozygous white cat, and black hair is dominant to white hair, what color would the offspring be?

    a.   all white
    b.   all black
    c.   some black cats and some white cats
    d.   each cat would have black and white hair

28. When two alleles of a gene are neither recessive or dominant to each other this is called

    a. a mutation
    b. incomplete dominance
    c. a purebred
    d. segregation

29. When a plant producing red flowers is crossed with a plant producing white flowers and the resulting offspring have pink flowers…this is an example of

    a. co-dominance
    b. recessive dominance
    c. incomplete dominance
    d. complete dominance

30. When a heterozygous black rabbit (Bb) is crossed with a white rabbit (bb), how many of their four offspring would you expect to be white?

    a. 4
    b. 3
    c. 2
    d. 1

Content Cluster-LIFE SCIENCE (EVOLUTION)

Objective: To introduce the topic of biological evolution and explain how it could account for the diversity of species over many generations.

Parent Tip: Evolution is the gradual change in hereditary traits over generations. For evolution to take place, something must upset the genetic balance of a population of organisms. Charles Darwin, the "father of evolution", believed that organisms with traits best suited to the environment in which they were living would survive and reproduce at a greater rate than organisms poorly suited to the environment. An example might be a bear in the arctic tundra with a heavy coat of fur compared to a bear with a very thin coat. This "survival of the fittest" or natural selection is the basis for the theory of evolution. When fossils are arranged according to their age, one can see how things have evolved or changed through the years. Other principles of evolution include: variation is present within a species, all organisms compete for natural resources, and organisms produce more offspring than can survive.

1. All the genes present in all of the individuals of a population are called the

   a. gene pool
   b. species pool
   c. selection pool
   d. mutation pool

2. A group of similar appearing individuals living in the same place at the same time is called

   a. a species
   b. a population
   c. an ecosystem
   d. a community

3. The preserved remains or evidence that a living thing once existed is called a (an)

   a. picture
   b. fossil
   c. isotope
   d. adaptation

4. The hardened sap of a tree that sometimes preserves insects that have become trapped is called

   a. tar
   b. petrified wood
   c. amber
   d. sedimentary rock

5. Parts of different organisms that are similar in structure are called

   a. vestigial structures
   b. homologous structures
   c. analogous structures
   d. comparative structures

6. The group of island off the coast of South America that is inhabited by the giant tortoise, marine iguana, and other life forms supporting the theory of evolution are called:

   a. the Hawaiian Islands
   b. the Philippine Islands
   c. the Galapagos Islands
   d. the Tahitian Islands

7. The book written by Charles Darwin to explain his theory of evolution was called

   a. The Beagle
   b. Natural Selection and Mutation
   c. The Origin of Species
   d. The Adaptation of Life

8. A physical trait that makes an organism better suited to its environment is called

   a. an adaptation
   b. a habitat
   c. a niche
   d. an expression

9. A species of a plant or animal that has completely disappeared is

   a. a threatened species
   b. an endangered species
   c. an extinct species
   d. an evolving species

10. Which of the following are use to provide evidence of the evolution of plants and animals?

    a.   comparing the DNA to look for chemical similarities between organisms
    b.   comparing the proteins that are found in different species
    c.   comparing the embryos of different organisms
    d.   all of the above

11. The term speciation means

    a.   the formation of a new species
    b.   the extinction of a species
    c.   the return of an extinct species
    d.   comparing two different species

12. What is a change in a gene or chromosome of an organism?

    a.   a translation
    b.   a mutation
    c.   natural selection
    d.   migration

13. What is the process in which one species evolves into several species, each which fills a different niche?`

    a.   adaptive radiation
    b.   mutation
    c.   migration
    d.   immigration

14. A species is defined as

    a.   a group of organisms that resemble one another but cannot produce offspring
    b.   a group of organisms that do not resemble one another but can produce offspring
    c.   a group of organisms that resemble one another and can produce offspring
    d.   none of the above

15. What are the differences between individuals in a population?

    a.   genetic recombination
    b.   variation
    c.   mutation
    d.   evolution

16. The habitat and the role that a species plays in that habitat is called a

   a. biome.
   b. niche.
   c. symbiosis.
   d. life style.

17. Which of the following is part of the theory of natural selection?

   a. there is variation within a species
   b. not all the offspring produced in each generation will survive
   c. individuals that survive and reproduce in greater numbers are those with the best variations
   d. all of the above

18. The theory that suggests that populations have remained genetically stable for long periods of time with brief periods or bursts of evolution is called

   a. gradualism.
   b. cross-over.
   c. punctuated equilibrium.
   d. isolationism.

19. Vestigial structures are those that

   a. are reduced in size and are often unused.
   b. are larger than normal and have become important to the life of the organism.
   c. are located in the anterior or head region of the organism.
   d. are identical to those of an unrelated species.

20. In looking at two different living species of plants or animals, one finds many similarities in the DNA and protein structure. If the similarities are close enough, one could conclude that

   a. one species came from the other.
   b. they both came from a common ancestor.
   c. they both changed by mutation.
   d. one is a clone of the other.

Content Cluster-EARTH SCIENCE

Objective: To help understand the evidence from rocks, fossils, and geology in presenting how life evolved on Earth.

Parent Tip: The Earth was thought to have formed approximately 4.6 billion years ago, with life starting in the ocean 1.5 billion years later. Much of what scientists know of the Earth's history is through the discovery of fossils and the scientific dating of the material. The movements of the Earth's continental and oceanic plates, major volcanic eruptions, and other catastrophic events have shaped the Earth's history and the life on it.

1. According to the "Big Bang" theory, the universe began

    a. about 2 billion years ago.
    b. as a dense cloud of matter that exploded 15 billion years ago.
    c. when two stars collided.
    d. about the same time as the Earth was formed.

2. Dinosaurs were the dominant life forms during which of Earth's eras?

    a. Cenozoic
    b. Mesozoic
    c. Precambrian
    d. Paleozoic

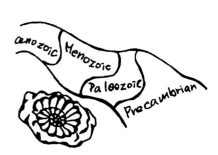

3. The idea that the continents have moved horizontally over time to there current locations is called

    a. continental drift.
    b. convection current.
    c. weathering.
    d. erosion.

4. Divergent boundaries in plate tectonics is where

    a. plates are moving apart.
    b. plates are moving together.
    c. plates slide past one another along faults.
    d. earthquakes occur.

5. The Earth's early atmosphere was composed of which group of materials?

   a. Oxygen, Hydrogen, and Carbon Dioxide
   b. Nitrogen, Hydrogen, and Oxygen
   c. Ammonia, Methane, Water and Hydrogen
   d. Oxygen, Methane, Water, and Hydrogen

6. Early Earth did not have life on land because of

   a. the lack of fresh water.
   b. the harmful ultraviolet rays of the sun.
   c. the lack of a food supply.
   d. all of the above

7. Most fossils are found in a type of rock called

   a. volcanic.
   b. granite.
   c. metamorphic.
   d. sedimentary.

8. You discover a fossil of seaweed and fish in one layer of rock. In a layer, just above these fossils you find an imprint of a fern leaf and tracks from a land animal. Assuming the rock has not been disturbed, what is the best conclusion.

   a. A forest was once here and is now covered by an ocean.
   b. The area has been underwater until recently.
   c. A freshwater lake has replaced a saltwater ocean.
   d. An ocean has been replaced by land long ago.

9. The ozone layer is a protective layer in the Earth's atmosphere created by

   a. the burning of fossil fuels.
   b. the evaporation of water.
   c. the release of carbon by decomposition.
   d. lightning and sunlight causing a change to oxygen molecules.

10. The geologic time scale began with the formation of the Earth approximately

   a. 46 thousand years ago.
   b. 4.6 million years ago.
   c. 4.6 billion years ago.
   d. 46 billion years ago.

11. Scientist believe the first living things on the Earth were

    a. small animals.
    b. land plants.
    c. fish.
    d. bacteria.

12. The disappearance of the dinosaurs was thought to be caused by

    a. predators that hunted and killed them for food.
    b. the sun's increase in temperature causing the evaporation of fresh water.
    c. an asteroid hitting the Earth and causing severe climate changes.
    d. disease that spread across the Earth.

13. The first Era in Earth's geologic time contains the largest amount of time, approximately 87% of the Earth's history. What is this era called?

    a. Mesozoic
    b. Paleozoic
    c. Cenozoic
    d. Precambrian

14. Name the supercontinent that eventually broke up into the continents we know today.

    a. Pangaea
    b. Atlantis
    c. Africanus
    d. Europa

15. A large asteroid or meteor hitting the Earth could cause

    a. the sun to be blocked by dust.
    b. plants and algae to stop photosynthesis.
    c. the temperature of the Earth to drastically drop.
    d. all of the above

16. Which of the following processes do some bacteria use to release oxygen?

    a. cell division
    b. respiration
    c. photosynthesis
    d. digestion

17. Which of the following is not a type of rock?

    a. metamorphic
    b. turquoise
    c. sedimentary
    d. igneous

18. Which of the following processes is part of the rock cycle?

    a. weathering and erosion
    b. heat and pressure
    c. compaction and cementation
    d. all of the above

19. Which would have the best chance of becoming a fossil?

    a. hard body parts and teeth
    b. internal digestive organs
    c. the skin or hair of an organism
    d. the brain and central nervous system

20. The principle of superposition states that in an undisturbed layer of rock

    a. the oldest rocks are on the top and become younger the deeper you go.
    b. the oldest rocks are on the bottom and become younger toward the top.
    c. rocks are generally a mixture of young and old caused by the constant movement of the Earth's crust.
    d. only rocks found in the high elevation can be used to determine age.

21. Relative dating techniques

    a. can give you an excellent data to determine the age of a fossil or rock.
    b. do not give you any information about the exact age of a specimen.
    c. can only compare the age of a specimen in relation to other fossils found in the same area (older than or younger than).
    d. both b and c are correct

22. The most accurate process for dating fossils, bones, or wood is

    a. radiometric dating (carbon-14, etc).
    b. relative dating.
    c. double dating.
    d. position in the rock layer.

23. What is the primary cause of the extinction of plant and animal species today?

    a. predation
    b. habitat destruction
    c. food poisoning
    d. competition

24. Which of the following could cause major climatic changes on the Earth?

    a. volcanic eruptions
    b. meteor or asteroid impacts
    c. increase carbon dioxide production
    d. all of the above

25. The age of mammals and the appearance of humans occurred in which era?

    a. Mesozoic
    b. Triassic
    c. Cenozoic
    d. Paleozoic

26. The Permian extinction is the boundary between the Paleozoic and Mesozoic eras. This is when almost 90% of the marine life on Earth became extinct. What is thought to have caused this catastrophic event?

    a. The merging of the continents to form Pangaea, which disturbed habitats.
    b. Massive volcanic eruptions causing global warming.
    c. Reduction of the oxygen available to the marine environment.
    d. all of the above

Cluster Content-STRUCTURE AND FUNCTION IN LIVING SYSTEMS

Parent Tip: Plants and animals have similar levels of organization. As with all living things, the structure and functions of different parts of these organisms are closely related. Processes including reproduction, movement, and the monitoring of the environment by the senses are all dependent upon systems. The failure of any part of the system can be harmful to the organism. Multicellular organisms, those made of many cells, have groups of similar cells working together to form tissues. Groups of different tissue work together to form an organ. Organs are combined to form systems. An example of an organ system is the digestive system. This system includes the organs of the stomach, small intestine, and large intestine as well as many large and small digestive glands. This system combines nervous tissue, muscle tissue, blood tissue, connective tissue, and glandular tissue together for a common function...digestion of food.

1. Which of the following is not one of the four basic tissues found in the human body?

    a. muscle tissue
    b. nervous tissue
    c. epithelial tissue
    d. cell wall tissue

2. The process by which the body's internal environment is kept stable is called

    a. regeneration.
    b. homeostasis.
    c. hypothermia.
    d. biogenesis.

3. Which of the following is not a system in the human body?

    a. integumentary
    b. immune
    c. endocrine
    d. biofeedback

4. Which of the following terms is the most complex?

    a. cell
    b. tissue
    c. organ
    d. system

5. Muscles and bones work together for support and movement. What is the structure that connects muscle to bone and keeps different muscles together?

    a. cartilage
    b. tendons
    c. valves
    d. joints

6. The muscles that are use for movement and are under voluntary control are called

    a. cardiac muscle.
    b. smooth muscle.
    c. skeletal muscle.
    d. all of the above

7. The joining of the egg and sperm in sexual reproduction is called

    a. fertilization.
    b. ovulation.
    c. menstruation.
    d. maturation.

8. The sex cells of animals are known as

    a. zygotes.
    b. ovum.
    c. sperm.
    d. both b and c are correct

9. The primary male reproductive organ is the

    a. ovary.
    b. fallopian tube.
    c. uterus.
    d. testes.

10. The organ that produces eggs in a female is called the

    a. ovary.
    b. testes.
    c. uterus.
    d. fallopian tube.

11. The organ in which the fetus develops in the female is called the

    a.   uterus.
    b.   urethra.
    c.   oviduct.
    d.   vagina.

12. Ovulation

    a.   is when the egg is released into the fallopian tube.
    b.   usually happens once each month in human females.
    c.   is controlled by hormones.
    d.   all of the above are true

13. The function of the placenta is to

    a.   nourish the developing embryo.
    b.   remove the waste materials from the embryo.
    c.   carry blood to the embryo through the umbilical cord.
    d.   all of these are correct

14. Which of the following substances can pass through the placenta to the fetus?

    a.   alcohol
    b.   tobacco smoke
    c.   drugs
    d.   all of the above

15. Sperm in the male animal is produced in the

    a.   ovary.
    b.   testes.
    c.   vas deferens.
    d.   uterus.

16. The umbilical cord

    a.   contains two arteries and one vein.
    b.   is the chief connection between the embryo and the mother's uterus.
    c.   is cut after birth and forms the "belly button".
    d.   all of the above are correct

17. In a flower, the male structure that contains the pollen and sperm is called the

    a. stamen.
    b. pistil.
    c. fruit.
    d. seed.

18. The first part of fertilization in a flowering plant is called

    a. pollination.
    b. ovulation.
    c. regeneration.
    d. germination.

19. The fruit of a plant

    a. contains seeds.
    b. is a ripened ovary.
    c. is a reproductive structure.
    d. all of these are correct

20 Pollination in flowering plants can be successfully accomplished by

    a. the wind.
    b. insects.
    c. bats.
    d. all of these

21. In some plants the pollen (carrying the sperm) of the plant is trapped by the stigma (part of the ovary) of the same plant. This is called

    a. cross pollination.
    b. self pollination.
    c. fertilization.
    d. mutation.

22. The seeds of flowering plants are dispersed by

    a. animals.
    b. wind.
    c. water.
    d. all of the above

23. The tear ducts that help lubricate the eye surface and help to remove foreign particles are called

    a.   endocrine glands
    b.   salivary glands
    c.   sebaceous glands
    d.   lacrimal glands

24. Which of the following structures are not found in the eye?

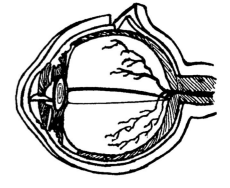

    a.   lens
    b.   iris
    c.   olfactory nerve
    d.   cornea

25. The retina is

    a.   the outer covering of the eye.
    b.   the innermost light-sensitive layer of the eye.
    c.   the muscle that gives the eye its color.
    d.   the opening in the eye for light.

26. The iris is

    a.   the structure of the eye that contains the photoreceptors.
    b.   the circular muscle that controls the opening of the pupil.
    c.   the structure that is seen as the "white of the eye".
    d.   the structure that focuses the light on the back part of the eye.

27. The part of the inner ear that is responsible for your sense of balance is called the

    a.   eardrum.
    b.   auditory canal.
    c.   Eustachian tube.
    d.   the semicircular canals.

28. In the inner ear, there is a fluid-filled tube containing little hairs that help transmit sound signals to the auditory nerve. This structure is called

    a.   the semicircular canals.
    b.   the anvil.
    c.   the cochlea.
    d.   the oval window.

29. The duct that connects the middle ear to the pharynx to equalize the pressure is called

    a. the trachea.
    b. the auditory canal.
    c. the Eustachian tube.
    d. the tympanic cavity.

30. Which of the following is not one of the three small bones in the middle ear that transmits vibrations to the inner ear?

    a. the malleus (hammer)
    b. the incus (anvil)
    c. the stapes (sturrup)
    d. the gluteus (saddle)

31. The eardrum separates

    a. the outer ear from the inner ear.
    b. the middle ear from the inner ear.
    c. the outer ear from the middle ear.
    d. the inner ear from the semicircular canals.

Content Cluster-PHYSICAL SCIENCE

Objective: To show some of the basic physical properties of matter and energy and how they can be applied to biological structures and functions

> **Parent Tip:** White light is a combination of all the different colors. These colors can be seen when separated by a prism or by water droplets in the air producing a rainbow. This white or visible light is only a small part of the electromagnetic spectrum released by the sun. The color of an object seen by the eye is the color of light reflected by the object. A red apple, absorbs all the colors in the visible spectrum except red, which is reflected into the eye.

1. Which of the following statements are true?

    a. visible light is the only part of the electromagnetic spectrum that you can see
    b. visible light is in the middle of the spectrum and cover a small range of light
    c. the wavelengths of infrared light are longer than visible light
    d. all of the above are true

2. Which of the following waves are not part of the electromagnetic spectrum?

    a. radio waves (TV, am and fm radio, short-wave)
    b. ultraviolet waves
    c. gamma waves
    d. ocean waves

3. As light travels from one medium (air), into another medium (water), what happens to light?

    a. it is refracted
    b. it travels in a straight line
    c. it changes color
    d. it disappears

4. When a wave of light strikes an object and bounces off, this is called?

    a. interference
    b. diffraction
    c. reflection
    d. refraction

5. The incident wave of a light is

   a. the incoming light wave hitting an object.
   b. the outgoing light wave that has hit an object.
   c. the wave of light that is absorbed by an object.
   d. visible light that is not seen.

6. The law of reflection states that

   a. the angle of incidence is greater than the angle of reflection.
   b. the angle of incidence is less than the angle of reflection.
   c. the angle of incidence is equal to the angle of reflection.
   d. an angle of incidence greater than ninety degrees cause no angle of reflection.

7. The refraction of visible light is the

   a. bending of light.
   b. shorting of the wavelength.
   c. lengthening of the wavelength.
   d. blocking of visible light.

8. If light waves change speed when they pass from one medium to another, what else happens to the light?

   a. It is refracted
   b. It is reflected
   c. It is scattered
   d. It changes colors

9. Which material absorbs or reflects all light?

   a. opaque material
   b. transparent material
   c. translucent material
   d. green material

10. What are the cells in the eye that are stimulated by color and allow you to see the detailed shapes of objects?

    a. rods
    b. cones
    c. both of these
    d. neither of these

11. What are the cells in the eye that are sensitive to dim light and are helpful in night vision?

    a.   rods
    b.   cones
    c.   bells
    d.   pigments

12. What is the opening in the eye that allows light to enter?

    a.   iris
    b.   pupil
    c.   lens
    d.   optic pore

13. When an object is seen as black

    a.   all wavelengths of visible light are being reflected.
    b.   all wavelengths of visible light are being absorbed.
    c.   black light is being reflected.
    d.   black light is being absorbed.

14. Red-green colorblindness, an inherited condition, means that

    a.   the individual cannot see the color red or green.
    b.   the individual can only see the color red or green.
    c.   the individual cannot distinguish the difference between the colors red and green.
    d.   red and green light are prevented from entering the eye.

15. The function of the lens in a microscope, camera, telescope and the human eye is to

    a.   focus the image.
    b.   reduce the amount of light.
    c.   increase the color of the light.
    d.   reduce the brightness of light.

16. Concave lenses

    a.   are thinner in the middle than at the edges.
    b.   are uses with other lenses in microscopes and cameras.
    c.   are used to correct nearsighted vision.
    d.   all of the above

17. A farsighted human eye focuses the image

    a.   on the top part of the retina.
    b.   behind the retina.
    c.   in front of the retina.
    d.   on the optic nerve.

18. Most plants are green in color. This means that

    a.   green light is being reflected into the eye.
    b.   green light is being absorbed by the plant.
    c.   all the colors of light but green are being reflected into the eye.
    d.   none of these statements are correct

19. In order for a lever to be functional, it needs a second part. This is called the

    a.   wheel.
    b.   pulley.
    c.   fulcrum.
    d.   wedge.

20. The hinge and ball and socket are mechanical devices that can be seen throughout the world. What system in the human body uses these devices to function?

    a.   circulatory system
    b.   nervous system
    c.   skeletal system
    d.   respiratory system

21. An example of a hinge joint is

    a.   the shoulder joint.
    b.   the elbow joint.
    c.   the ankle joint.
    d.   the hip joint.

22. A muscle that extends a joint is called a

    a.   flexor muscle.
    b.   relaxor muscle.
    c.   contractile muscle.
    d.   extensor muscle.

23. To provide motion in animals, most skeletal muscles

    a. contract at the same time.
    b. move bones in many different directions.
    c. work in pairs, with one contracting as the other relaxes.
    d. work independently and without voluntary control.

24. The heart of an animal generates pressure by contracting. What are the structures in this organ that prevent the blood from going the wrong direction?

    a. arteries
    b. veins
    c. valves
    d. capillaries

25. Which of the following blood vessels carry blood away from the heart?

    a. arteries
    b. veins
    c. venules
    d. the lymphatic tubules

26. The pressure in the circulatory system that is caused by the ventricles contracting is

    a. systolic pressure.
    b. diastolic pressure.
    c. the second number when recording blood pressure (140/80).
    d. less when the individual is exercising.

27. High blood pressure is dangerous and is known as

    a. atherosclerosis.
    b. hemophilia.
    c. arteriosclerosis.
    d. hypertension.

28. The sounds that are heard when you listen to the heart beat are caused by

    a. blood rushing in and out.
    b. the muscle beating rhythmically.
    c. the pacemaker stimulating the heart muscle.
    d. the valves of the heart closing.

29. What is the muscular pumping chambers of the heart?

    a.   atria
    b.   aorta
    c.   vena cava
    d.   ventricles

30. Which of the following blood vessels are under the least pressure?

    a.   arteries
    b.   capillaries
    c.   veins
    d.   all of these vessels have the same pressure